Architecture in Perspective

12th Annual International Competition of Architectural Perspectivists

The American Society of Architectural Perspectivists

**First published in the
United States of America by:**
Rockport Publishers, Inc.
33 Commercial Street
Gloucester, Massachusetts
01930-5089
Telephone: (508) 282-9590
Fax: (508) 283-2742

**Distributed to the book
trade and art trade in
the United States by:**
North Light Books, an imprint of
F & W Publications
1507 Dana Avenue
Cincinnati, Ohio 45207
Telephone: (800) 289-0963

Other Distribution by:
Rockport Publishers, Inc.
Gloucester, Massachusetts
01930-5089

ISBN 1-56496-411-6

10 9 8 7 6 5 4 3 2 1

Manufactured in China

Contents

Editor
Gordon S. Grice OAA, MRAIC

Designer
John Deputy, MetroDesign

ASAP wishes to thank the following individuals whose
dedication to their tasks went far beyond the call of duty:

Jurors: Raymond G. Post FAIA (chairman), Attila Hejja,
E. Fay Jones FAIA
Alexandra Lee, ASAP Executive Director
Charlie Manus, ASAP President
Steve Oles FAIA, ASAP co-founder and Member-at-large
Connie Hendrix

**We would especially like to thank Otis Elevator
Company for their continuing encouragement
and financial support.**

Foreword

Illustrators share with their patrons the deeply personal rewards of creative work. Members of the American Society of Architectural Perspectivists share with each other the many advantages of mutual learning, mutual experience, and friendships, which make them better professionals than they might otherwise be.

For these and many other reasons, I've always considered architectural illustration to be one of the best jobs anyone could hope to have.

None of this means, of course, that ASAP members should be entirely satisfied with themselves or complacent about their organization. On the contrary, ASAP has barely scratched the surface of its ability to help perspectivists grow their talents, skills, and businesses, and its potential to support progress in the broader fields of rendering and visual expression. ASAP's goal should be to move to the forefront of professional organizations whose members enjoy direct benefits from their membership and participation in group events and activities.

This can be accomplished by increasing organization and sponsorship of seminars and demonstrations from which every illustrator, beginner or veteran, can learn. At the same time, ASAP should strive to help its members achieve a fuller understanding of what they do and why they do it. Renderers do not merely give form and color to an idea. While some illustrations have only minutes to communicate their crucial message, others hang as fine art in prestigious places.

Architecture in Perspective is ASAP's annual artistic audit of the profession. Entries come from all over the world and are submitted by professionals and amateurs, students and professors, beginners and seasoned practitioners. No allowance is made for a work's original purpose, length of time required for execution, tightness of deadline, or size of budget. Artistic excellence is the only criterion for selection. While our organization has much to accomplish in coming years, our members can be justifiably proud of their individual accomplishments, evident on the pages of this book.

Charlie Manus
President, American Society of Architectural Perspectivists

Charlie Manus
President, American Society of Architectural Perspectivists

Architecture in Perspective 12 Venue Schedule

Feature image from the AIP Call-for-entries Poster: The Peabody Hotel, Memphis, Tennessee
Architects: Walter W. Alschuler; Illustrator: S. Chester Danforth (1925), Image Courtesy of The Peabody Hotel

Askew, Nixon & Ferguson Architects
Memphis, Tennessee
October 18–November 16, 1997

Mount Ida College
Newton, Massachusetts
November 28, 1997–January 2, 1998

The Octagon
The Museum of the American Architectural Foundation
Washington, DC
January 15–June 30, 1998

AIA National Convention
San Francisco, California
Special Members Exhibit
May 14–17, 1998

Chicago Architecture Foundation
Chicago, Illinois
Tentative
July–September 1998

Introduction

The jurying process ensures that every *Architecture in Perspective* show has its own distinct personality. This process is, in turn, affected by an infinite number of variables, including the nature of the submissions, the characteristics of the jury (individually and in concert), the judging venue, world events, and even the weather.

"I Don't Care if the Sun Don't Shine"
Title of a song written by M. David and recorded by Elvis Presley at the Sun Recording Studio in Memphis, from The Sun Sessions *CD, New York: BGM Music, 1987*

You can imagine what sort of day it must have been in Memphis forty-two and a half years ago, when Elvis recorded those words—not unlike the conditions on Valentine's Day, 1997, when the group of us gathered in the same city to adjudicate the twelfth annual *Architecture in Perspective* exhibition. Memphis, just recovering from a snowstorm, was cold and gray. But, our task, like Elvis's, didn't require sunshine.

Besides, the gray skies made it all the easier to sit inside and concentrate. A dim room is ideal for slide-viewing. Last year, Boston; this year, Memphis; it has become almost traditional for the sky to be dark and stormy for the annual judging. It's a good sign.

"Where are the pylons, and the obelisks, and the avenues of sphinxes? Where, in short, is Memphis?"
Clayton, P.A., The Rediscovery of Ancient Egypt—Artists and Travellers in the 19th Century, *London: Thames and Hudson.*

Memphis is part of the great American heartland. It is, for one thing, "America's distribution centre": the vast Federal Express central headquarters are located here. Memphis is also the cradle and nursery for a lot of North American popular music, and Beale Street continues that tradition. Graceland is in Memphis. Reverend Al Greene's church is in Memphis. Cybill Shepherd's house is in Memphis. And, let's not forget, the world's first supermarket chain, Piggly Wiggly, started in Memphis. Sense of place exerts a subtle influence on the judging process.

"I also heard other things at Memphis in conversation with the priests of Hephaestus."
Herodotus, Book Two, Chapter III (Herodotus was a Greek historian of the 5th century B.C. Hephaestus was the Greek god of handicrafts whose temple was a landmark in ancient Memphis.)

The assembly of the *Architecture in Perspective* show is a work of art in itself and, just as the individual pieces reflect the nature of the artists that created them, the show also reflects the characteristics of the artists that created it: the AIP jury. This year's jury, the inspired creation of current ASAP President Charlie Manus, was a particularly fine one. Each of the jurors has a distinguished career and a sense of aesthetic sensibilities unique to himself. Attila Hejja is an internationally renowned commercial artist whose honors include a gold medal from the Society of Illustrators. Raymond G. (Skipper) Post Jr. FAIA, is the past president of the national AIA and a tireless advocate for the betterment of the profession of architecture. E. Fay Jones FAIA, is a living legend, recipient of the AIA Gold Medal, and an ACSA Distinguished Professor.

Graceland

Together these three august gentlemen formed a cohesive group: highly focused, thoughtful but convivial, committed to their own ideals but respectful of others. The result of their deliberation is a show with remarkable strength and unlike any other. Particularly notable is the degree to which new faces have replaced old. For all their wisdom, the priests of Hephaestus could not have done a better job.

"Don't make it too damn complicated."
Sam Phillips, founder of Sun Records, Memphis, 1955, advising Elvis Presley's sideman Scotty Moore, quoted by Peter Guralnick in the liner notes for The Sun Sessions *CD, New York: BGM Music, 1987*

Sam Phillips's immortal words were echoed by the jurors of AIP 12. Time and again during the course of the proceedings, one of the jurors would remark on the importance of simplicity. Referring to Steve Parker's Sketch Category winner, Attila said: "When you can simplify and do it well, it's a thing of beauty. There's virtue in simplicity."

This philosophy was also reflected in the large number of computer-generated images selected. "Simple" may not be the best way to describe the computer drawing process, but the result, when done well, can be pleasantly free from obvious sophistication: elemental and factual. No drawing displays these characteristics better than the Ferriss Prize-winning drawing by Advanced Media Design. The strength of composition and simplicity of execution is a testament to the skill of the artists in guiding the digital process toward the highest analog standards.

"A few scattered ruins are all that is left of Memphis...."
Carpiceci, A.C., Art and History of Egypt—5000 years of Civilization, *Florence: Bonechi, 1994*

Well, that may be true of the Egyptian Memphis, but of the Tennessee Memphis, a fine monument remains, in the form of *Architecture in Perspective 12*.

Jury Report

Every year at the national AIA convention, I go directly to the ASAP exhibit and spend more time there than on all the other hundreds of displays on the exhibition floor simply because the work is so extraordinary—so magnificent. Serving on the jury for the ASAP *Architecture in Perspective* exhibition was one of the most enjoyable moments that emanated from my service as 1996 president of the American Institute of Architects.

Because of my great admiration and respect for the capabilities of the ASAP members, it was a special treat to be invited to serve as the chair of the jury, and it was an added pleasure to serve with two eminently qualified jurors: E. Fay Jones FAIA, and Attila Hejja. I have known Fay for several years and had known of his architectural work for some time, before actually meeting him at about the time he received his AIA Gold Medal, one of the most prestigious architectural awards in the world. I met Attila for the first time at the AIP jury, but I was immediately impressed by his own artistic works and by his ability to judge the submissions in a unique way that was both personal and informed by a profound knowledge of artistic process. Both Fay and Attila were excellent jurists and their reasoned deliberations helped to guide me in making my own assessments. I thank them both for their wisdom and support.

Since I have not served as an adjudicator of renderings before, I cannot compare this year's submissions to those of any other year. I can only say that I was struck by the extremely high quality of most of the 540 slides. My first thought, after viewing all of the entries was: how in the world would we narrow the selection to so few pieces. It never became an easy task.

For an architect, it takes an extreme twist of the mind to judge renderings and not the buildings that they portray. This leads to a further dilemma: can the accustomed judgment parameters be set aside, so that poor architecture doesn't cloud the appreciation of the rendering? For me, this took some effort and reminded me of the question asked by last year's jury chair, Bill Mitchell: should an artist strive to enhance poor architecture? My answer would have to be that the artist is not a critic, but an advocate, portraying a building in a true, if enhanced, form and setting, without dishonest representation.

Styles and techniques of rendering, special treatments, and and other considerations change through time, and that is as it should be. But, as in architecture, good taste endures longer than trendy styles. A beautiful and simply executed pen or pencil drawing is timeless. The same is true of a good basic watercolor painting. Simple is best.

Sometimes drawings become sophisticated in ways that are trendy to the point of cliché. It has been noted that last year's drawings seemed plagued by seagulls (the year before, it was searchlights). This year, there were moons: full moons, new moons, moons in the daytime, and moons at night. In the late fifties and sixties, there were the aerial perspectives looking down the wing of an airplane or through the open door of a helicopter. To magnify the effect, birds and kites were added. Artists must be careful to be innovators and not duplicators. An innocent cliché can spoil an otherwise unique work of art.

Trends are not necessarily all bad. Some, like the use of computers in drawing, are deep-rooted and promise to be long-lasting. Computer-aided rendering can be realistic to a degree that is difficult to achieve in hand-done rendering, and there is certainly a demand for this type of work. But the difference between computer rendering and hand-done rendering is frequently difficult to identify and even more difficult to define. I know that this is the subject of ongoing discussion at ASAP, but it might be a good idea to try to separate the two for the purposes of judging in future exhibitions.

The drawings that we have selected for exhibition are extremely diverse in style and technique, but among the six award winners, there are some unexpected similarities.The Hugh Ferriss Memorial Prize goes to Advanced Media Design for a striking study of shade, shadow, and contrast in a competion entry for a World War II Memorial—a dramatic and effective portrayal of a powerful space. The Formal Category winner, the Carolinas Stadium by Dick Sneary, also depicts an entry with strong classical forms under dramatic lighting conditions, presenting a strong sense of attraction. The elegant Informal Category winner by Steve Parker renders the classical forms of the St. Louis Justice Center in a much more subtle and restrained way, but lighting is used to reinforce the strong simple proportions.

Raymond G. Post FAIA (chairman)

E. Fay Jones FAIA

Attila Hejja

Of the three Juror's Award winners, two depict railway stations, and one shows a new embassy building. Attila Hejja was immediately attracted to the open and light-filled illustration of the Frankfurt Hauptbanhof 2010 by Martin J. Newton. Fay Jones preferred the subtle and evocative play of grays with only mildly used colors depicting the railway station Hollands Spoor by Theo van Leur. For my own Juror's Award, I found the use of siting and context in Douglas E. Jamieson's United States Embassy competition drawing irresistible.

In addition to thanking jury members Fay Jones and Attila Hejja, I would also like to thank the staff members and hosts. It was a long journey for all the jury members. My own trip was lengthened by airline schedule failures, broken airplanes, and a midnight arrival. Attila suffered a similar fate. But we were rewarded with attentive support and totally adept preparations, the lack of which would have been frustrating, given the 540 slides to be viewed. Alexandra Lee, executive director of ASAP, had the slides and paperwork well orchestrated. Charlie Manus and Connie Hendrix made all the physical arrangements to ensure that the judging went smoothly and that we were comfortable, entertained, and well fed. Connie was assisted during the judging by editor Gordon Grice and, of course, Steve Oles FAIA, whose tremendous depth of experience and vibrant energy added greatly to the proceedings. Without this assistance, our arduous task, which covered about 12 hours, could have lasted days. Thank you all.

Finally, congratulations to the winners and to all ASAP entrants who clearly add a significant measure of quality and added value to the architectural profession.

Raymond G. Post FAIA

Charlie Manus's Union Avenue office: the judging venue

Skipper Post, Steve Oles and E. Fay Jones (l to r)

Hugh Ferriss Memorial Prize

For his entry in the World War II Monument competition for the Washington Mall, architect Friedrich St. Florian asked his renderers, Advanced Media Design, to provide a series of drawings that would be "subtle but powerful." The request was a simple one, but this combination of qualities is not easily achieved.

The American architect/illustrator Hugh Ferriss was a master at combining subtlety and power. His body of work constitutes an encyclopedia on the many ways that these attributes can reinforce each other to create striking architectural imagery. It is especially fitting that Advanced Media Design has been awarded the Hugh Ferriss Memorial Prize, because, like Hugh Ferriss himself, they manage to achieve this combination in starkly beautiful architectural drawing.

Not surprisingly, the three illustrators of Advanced Media Design, Jon Kletzien, Richard Dubrow, and James Kuhn, are admirers of the work of Hugh Ferriss and are occasional collaborators with ASAP founder Steve Oles whose own work is strongly evocative of Ferriss (Steve was the Ferriss winner in AIP 11). What is unusual about Advanced Media's response to the distinctively "analog" Ferriss tradition is that they do their renderings on a computer.

For anyone who believes that computer rendering is an exercise best suited to technicians and that only hand-done rendering can be considered true art, the World War II Monument drawing provides a convincing refutation. Not only does it lack the clinical, overly detailed "high-tech" look of much computer rendering, it also incorporates many features that are more characteristic of manual drawing. The forms are soft and full. The lighting is dramatic but smoothly molded and free of the glare and gimmicks for which some software is famous. The one possible concession to digital effects is the elaborate reflective ground-plane, but this element is made so subtle by the carefully controlled lighting that it registers almost subliminally, and the other surfaces are treated in a light-absorbing matte finish.

Richard Dubrow explains the team's approach to computer drawing by saying, "computers are an illustration tool. We're not its tool—it's our tool." Like any drawing medium, a computer responds only to the guidance that it is given. Advanced Media is very clear in wanting to retain as much aesthetic control as possible. "Style should not be dictated by a computer program," says Dubrow.

To ensure this aesthetic control, a variety of programs were used to create the image, each with its own strengths. The base model was created by James Kuhn using AutoCad, a popular and ubiquitous program among architects and designers. The rendering was then performed by Dubrow and Kletzien using 3D Studio, another popular and versatile program. Finally, to add spontaneity and a hand-done finish to the piece, Hi Res QFX was used to modify the lighting effects and to soften the scanned-in figures, sky, and landscape. The resulting image seems to combine all the strengths of three distinct forms of expression—computer drawing, hand rendering, and photography—in one seamless image.

Fay Jones called the drawing "a powerful rendering." The other jurors agreed whole heartedly. Attila Hejja added, "I love this drawing." Probably the jurors of the memorial competition in Washington felt the same way, for while Advanced Media Design was in the process of winning the Ferriss Prize, Friedrich St. Florian was named the winner of the World War II Monument Competition. We are honored to present such a beautiful and distinguished drawing as the feature drawing of *Architecture in Perspective 12.*

Advanced Media Design

Project: World War II Memorial, Evening, Colonnade View, Washington, DC
Architect: Friedrich St. Florian
Client: American Battle Monuments Commission
Computer generated, 15 x 24

Formal Category Award

Light plays an extremely important role in an architectural illustration. In all of the six award winners, and in many of the other show selections, lighting forms a critical element in the composition of the drawing. This year's Formal Category winner is a watercolor rendering by Dick Sneary of Kansas City, Mo., of the new Carolinas Stadium in Charlotte, N.C., for the Carolina Panthers football team. Dick has imbued the building with a warm glow that floods the entry with light that seems to leak out the top of the open stadium as well. The bold forms flanking the arched entry are presented in dark silhouette against the illumination from within.

Juror Attila Hejja was unwavering in his praise: "This is a delightful piece; everything is done right." Attila went on to praise the subtlety of the presentation, referring in particular to the way in which normally overdone elements (the flags and flagpoles, for example) are actually underplayed: "What he doesn't show is as important as what he does show."

Another distinctive quality of the painting is its bold composition. The page is divided almost in half, horizontally, with the dark sky in the top half and the building in the bottom. Interest and a strong focal center are created in this bottom half by presenting the symmetrical scheme asymmetrically, so that the entry is to the left of center and the stadium curves back into the picture plane on the right. Diminishing figures and silhouetted trees lead the eye from the bottom margin into the drawing's focus.

In preparing the drawing, Dick was especially inspired by the building's landscaping treatment. Owner Jerry Richardson had been sure to allow a generous landscaping budget in order to guarantee that the Carolinas Stadium wouldn't suffer the fate of many other stadiums: a well-designed facility surrounded by a huge poorly-designed expanse of concrete and asphalt. Landscape Architect Peter Schaunt provided a strong organic element, including some live oaks to buffer the base of the building. This drawing of the stadium is one of about two dozen that Dick has prepared for the designers, HOK Sports Facilities Group, Kansas City Mo., including about half a dozen landscape sketches.

Dick Sneary has also been well represented in previous AIP exhibitions, including a Juror's Award in AIP 8. An interior view of the Carolinas Stadium appeared in the *AIP 10* Designated Entries section.

Dick Sneary
Sneary Architectural Illustration

Project: Carolinas Stadium, Charlotte, NC
Architect: HOK Sports Facilities Group
Watercolor, 7 x 11

Informal (Sketch) Category Award

The AIP 12 jurors shared one firm belief from the beginning: simplicity and economy are the hallmarks of superior rendering.

" When you can simplify and do it well, it's a thing of beauty. There's virtue in simplicity."
Juror Attila Hejja

Steve Parker's understated pencil and watercolor sketch of the St. Louis City Justice Center provided an excellent example of this tenet. Like all of the six award-winning drawings in AIP 12, the color palette is intentionally limited: blues and creams, cool against warm, but with an overall brightness. Steve felt that a complex or bold color scheme would betray the drawing's basic simplicity and decided instead to rely on good color organization, a well-conceived shade and shadow study, and some bold compositional elements to tie the drawing together.

A major concern was the overshadowing aspect of the tall Eighth District Federal Courts Building in the background. Where the foreground building helps to frame the subject, the taller court building, because of its location, would compete with it. The tightly cropped block of sky helps to retain the focus on the subject and establishes an interesting rhythm in the skyline.

The idea of using a pencil-line drawing as the basis for the drawing came from the client, Joe Kuss with the Board of Public Services of St. Louis. The board was working against an extremely tight deadline and wished to put together a black-and-white presentation booklet in advance of the completed sketch. So Steve prepared a small pencil drawing on linen that was given to the client after being enlarged onto watercolor paper. Barring any tragic accidents or errors, watercolor renderings can sometimes benefit from a short deadline. That is certainly the case with this drawing.

" I think this is a delightful sketch. It's difficult to simplify and interpret at the same time. I think he's interpreted what we see nicely."
Juror Attila Hejja

Attila's statement helps to clarify the appeal that sketches have and the reason that the AIP shows continue to encourage the submission of sketches, even to the point of giving them their own category. Unfortunately, too often design professionals equate sophistication with excellence and simplicity with inferiority and ignore the value of simple drawings. With increasing frequency, as computer renderings become more common, illustrators are being asked by their clients to prepare quick sketches in lieu of elaborate renderings. The result can be seen in the fine work selected by the jury for the Informal Category and epitomized by this exceptional work by Steve Parker.

Steve Parker
Parker Studios

Project: St. Louis City Justice Center, St. Louis, MO
Architect: Hellmuth, Obata + Kassabaum with Kennedy Associates
Client: Joe Kuss with the Board of Public Services of St. Louis
Watercolor, 15 x 21

Juror's Awards

"This is going to be harder than I thought."
Skipper Post, after the first round

So attuned to one another were this year's jurors, that their Juror's Award selections share many common features. As their personal favorites, jurors Attila Hejja, Fay Jones, and Skipper Post selected three low-rise buildings—two railway stations and an embassy—all with evocative lighting and skillfully restrained color palettes and, coincidentally, all European projects located within 350 miles of each other.

Attila Hejja has gained considerable renown in creating images of high-tech subjects for the US space program and for a variety of covers and illustrations for popular technology magazines. Paradoxically, he admitted to an aversion to computer imagery that gradually evaporated under the influence of the large number of excellent computer-generated images submitted for AIP 12.

In referring to his Juror's Award selection, he stated: "I have to confess a bias against computer art on principle, but I'm slowly coming around to admitting that I shouldn't have one. This is every bit as good as anything that I've ever seen done by hand."

The illustration of the Frankfurt Hauptbahnhof 2010 by Martin Newton of Berlin, Germany, is a dynamic image of a railway station platform showing people and trains in suspended motion while a large skylight and window wall flood the interior with glorious sunlight. In Hejja's words, "You get a sense of temperature, time of day, even time of year. You can almost hear the echo-sounds of a public place. This, in my opinion, is what good art is all about; it gives you a very strong sense of presence." The image focuses on architectural space rather than form—a space that tends to project beyond the confines of the flanking walls of tiered arcades and through the light curved trusses supporting the skylight, reinforcing the transient nature of the Bahnhof. Juror Hejja remarked that the artist displays "a degree of sensitivity and understands light and perspective," making this "the most elegant piece in the show."

The illustration selected by Fay Jones for his Juror's Award depicts a similar subject, a railway station, but in a very different way. Dutch renderer Theo van Leur's watercolor image of the proposed railway station Hollands Spoor shows an exterior view as opposed to Newton's interior. Where Newton's image is filled with daylight, van Leur shows a brooding crepuscular sky. The light from the station's interior seems to offer warmth and comfort.

"There's something about train stations and weepy skies that go very well together," Fay said, and added, "it depicts more than just a building; it depicts a feeling....the mood and atmospheric effects are magical." Where the Hauptbahnhof promises happy arrivals, the railway station is more reminiscent of sad departures or possibly the disorientation one feels arriving in a strange city after travelling all day.

Fay Jones was also impressed by van Leur's gentle technique, involving "wonderful gradations of subtle velvety colors that flow beautifully." Much of the drawing's appeal is, in fact, due to the artist's restrained color palette, moving smoothly from cool gray at the top and bottom to pale yellows in the center, without any bright colors to destroy the mood.

In summation, Fay said that the van Leur drawing "represents a very special realm of art. I have nothing but high praise for this artist."

In the final Juror's Award selection, that of Skipper Post, a gray sky again creates a mood of intrigue. The subject of the painting is the new U.S. embassy building in Berlin, so a little intrigue might be expected. Douglas E. Jamieson's watercolor of Moore Ruble Yudell's winning competition entry presents a very compelling sense of atmospheric texture. The sky is gray-blue and visibility close to the ground is slightly restricted, suggesting the lifting of dew in the early morning. The building's walls are more brightly lit at the top, an effect that might be created by a rising sun. The foreground trees are bare and, despite the dim light, there are a number of pedestrians, dressed warmly and walking briskly. The ground is clear of fallen leaves or snow. It is late winter. Skipper Post was terse but clear in his praise of the drawing: "This is one of, if not the best, in the show."

Doug Jamieson's work is by now familiar to AIP audiences. For his debut in AIP 7, he won the Hugh Ferriss Prize, and he has appeared in every show since that time, winning another Juror's Award in AIP 9.

The *Architecture in Perspective* jury process is unlike that of most other award programs in that jurors are normally selected from fields other than architectural illustration and, although they may have sat on many juries, they have probably never adjudicated architectural renderings before. With only the briefest of introductions to the process and almost no information about the drawings, the three are asked to set a new benchmark for the profession. For ASAP this represents an annual rejuvenation and redefinition. While the process still has some glitches, it has been remarkably successful in helping the Society to achieve its goals: establishing a forum for discussion about architectural drawing, raising awareness concerning such drawing, and providing encouragement for illustrators to continue to improve the quality of their work.

Martin J. Newton
Archimation

Project: Frankfurt Hauptbahnhof 2010, Frankfurt, Germany
Architect: von Gerkan, Marg + Partner
Client: Deutsche Bahn AG
Computer, 20 x 24

Theo van Leur
Theo van Leur Architectuur Presentaties B.V.

Project: Railway station "Hollands Spoor," The Hague, The Netherlands
Architect: Theo Fikkers, B.V. Articon
Client: N.S. Stations B.V.
Watercolor and airbrush on board, 18 x 32

Douglas E. Jamieson

Project: United States Embassy Competition, Berlin, Germany
Architect: Moore Ruble Yudell
Client: Moore Ruble Yudell
Watercolor , 18 x 24

Awards of Excellence

The *Architecture in Perspective 12* traveling exhibition consists of the six top award winners shown on the preceding pages and the 51 drawings and paintings on the following pages. All have been selected by the three distinguished judges to be the best from among the 540 works submitted.

This year ASAP continues the tradition of using only two categories of submission, Formal and Informal, although the discussion about increasing this number builds in intensity. Over the past decade, numerous proposals by members and jurors have been brought forward and debated at length. But every system has its flaws and it appears that simple is still best.

Making a particularly strong bid for a category of their own are the computer-aided renderings. The number of computer-rendered submissions increases every year and this year, for the first time, the Ferriss Prize has been awarded to a computer rendering. How can computer drawings continue to be judged beside hand-done illustrations? The necessity to do so can be explained by two facts.

First, computers are used at some stage in the preparation of most architectural renderings today, frequently even in sketches. So a decision must be made as to where to draw the line (as it were). If you wish to distinguish drawings whose final form is on a screen, rendered digitally, from those whose final form is on a hard surface and rendered "by hand," there are still sufficient hybrid products (hand-done drawings scanned into a computer and rendered with media programs, computer line-drawings printed onto art paper and hand-colored, computer collages, etc.) to make the distinction a very artificial one.

Second, ASAP has managed in its twelve years to preserve the supremacy of content over form when it comes to architectural art. The Society bridles at the thought (as has been often suggested) of separating drawings based on technique, such as watercolor or mixed media. To do so would be to draw attention to how a rendering has been made—to remove some of the magic—and reduce rather than enhance the significance of the accomplishment. In a work of art, technique ought to be transparent, like glass in a window. In this discussion, the computer is a large paintbrush. In the hands of an artist, art will result, in the hands of a technician, a computer drawing.

The distinction between formal and informal drawings is made for two reasons: first, to encourage illustrators to submit drawings regardless of their degree of polish and realism, and second, to free the judges from the necessity to judge all drawings by the same criteria. Although entrants are required to designate in which category their work belongs, jurors are free to recategorize drawings as they see fit. In the following pages, drawings are ordered alphabetically by artist, with formal and informal intermixed.

Formal Category Winners

Formal drawings are those that are dimensionally accurate, graphically descriptive, and tending toward a "realistic" representation. At times drawings that demonstrate none of these characteristics, but are done in a careful or deliberate way, are also deemed to be formal drawings. The Awards of Excellence include highly realistic perspective renderings, as well as orthographic drawings and collages; drawings that are client-commissioned along with self-commissioned works; images executed on a computer, and renderings done by hand in a wide variety of media.

Informal Category Winners

Informal drawings, or sketches, are considered to be anything that doesn't fall neatly into the Formal category. Typically these drawings are the result of a technique rapidly applied that captures the essence of an idea, often before it has been clearly articulated in the mind of the creator. Understandably, sketches are frequently the product of the building designer, who may or may not be a professional illustrator. But there are any number of other kinds of drawings that the jury or entrant might qualify as informal, including experimental and exploratory drawings, abstract works, collages, and anything else that might be considered "informal."

To fully appreciate the artwork reproduced on these pages, there is really no substitute for seeing the exhibition in person. In this catalogue, you will find a partial list of venues, which is prone to changes and additions. You are encouraged to call ASAP for current information concerning AIP 12 and future shows.

Addresses and telephone numbers of the award winners can be found in the Membership Directory, starting on page 136.

Jim Anderson
Anderson Illustration Associates

Project: The Livingston, Madison, WI
Architect: Cunningham Welch Design Group
Client: Cunningham Welch Design Group
Watercolor, 9 x 6
Informal category

Richard C. Baehr AIA
Architectural Rendering

Project: Proposed New York Stock Exchange Building, New York, NY
Architect: Kohn Pedersen Fox Associates P.C.
Client: Donald J. Trump
Tempera, 19 x 37
Formal category

Alexander Ballings
7ARTS visuals bv.

Project: City Hall Amsterdam-noord, The Netherlands
Architect: Frans Kooyman (Van Overhage Architecten)
Client: Blauwhoed projectontwikkeling
Airbrush and pencil, 24 x 36
Formal category

Frank Bartus
Genesis Studios

Project: Firstate Tower, Orlando, FL
Architect: VOA Associates
Gouache on airbrush-enhanced photo print, 19 x 19
Formal category

Luis Blanc

Project: Proposed One Rockefeller Plaza, New York, NY
Architect: Kevin Kennon
Client: Kohn Pedersen Fox Associates P.C.
Black Prismacolor pencil, 20 x 11

Informal category

Nicholas J. Buccalo AIA
The Drawing Studio

Project: Lujiazui—Itochu Development Building, Pudong, Shanghai, China
Architect: Sydness Architects P.C.
Client: Lujiazui—Itochu Development Corporation
Digital, 15 x 12
Formal category

Mike Burroughs

Project: Samsung Retail Interiors, Seoul, South Korea
Architect: Callison Architecture
Client: Samsung
Ink and acrylic, 18 x 24
Formal category

Li Chen
Cyber Expression LLC

Project: Executive Room
Architect: Keogh Design
Client: AEA Investors
Computer rendering, 20 x 34
Formal category

Richard Chenoweth AIA
Architectural Watercolors

Project: Monumental Screen, Bureau of Engraving and Printing, Washington, DC
Architect: Weinstein Associates Architects
Client: Bureau of Engraving and Printing, Treasury Department
Watercolor, 13 x 18
Formal category

Frank M. Costantino
F. M. Costantino

Project: Oceanario de Lisboa, Lisbon, Portugal
Architect: Cambridge Seven & Associates
Client: Cambridge Seven & Associates
Watercolor, 14 x 24
Formal category

Elizabeth A. Day

Project: Swiss RE America, U.S. Headquarters, Armonk, NY
Architect: Schnabli, Amman, Ruchat with Steven Fong
Client: Swiss RE America
Watercolor, 12 x 16
Formal category

Angelo De Castro

Project: Quartier an der Museumsinsel, Berlin, Germany
Architect: Steffen Lehmann & Partner; Arata Isozaki & Associates
Client: Hanseatica Unternehmensgruppe Deutsche Immobilien Anlagegesellschaft mbh
Airbrush, 8 x 16
Formal category

Gilbert Gorski AIA
Gorski & Associates P.C.

Project: Porta del Rientro
Architect: Gilbert Gorski AIA
Client: Self-commissioned
Watercolor and color pencil, 13 x 10
Formal category

Bei Guan
Bay Illustration Studio

Project: Global Building, Bellevue, WA
Architect: Mulvanny Partnership/Kappler Thomas Harkey
Client: SU Development
Watercolor and inkline, 22 x 30
Informal category

Headrick Chase & Associates

Project: Sun City Grand/Social Building, Surprize, AZ
Architect: The Dahlin Group
Client: Del Webb Home Construction
Digital, 18 x 33
Formal category

William G. Hook
W. G. Hook, Architectural Illustration

Project: Harborview Hospital Study, Seattle, WA
Client: Self-commissioned
Transparent watercolor, 6 x 2
Informal category

Suns S. K. Hung
Sun & Associates

Project: Four Times Square, New York, NY
Architect: Fox & Fowle Architects
Client: The Durst Organization
Pen and ink with watercolor on Bainbridge board, 32 x 24
Formal category

Takuji Kariya
RIYA Co., Ltd.

Project: Hotel Azusa, Nagano, Japan
Architect: Architects Z
Watercolor on Arches board 18 x 26
Formal category

Young H. Ki, KIA
Young H. Ki & Associates

Project: Hanjoong Industries & Information Center, Seoul, South Korea
Architect: Anderson & Oh with Haenglim Architects
Color pencil, pen and ink, 26 x 19
Formal category

Joseph C. Knight
Knight Architects

Project: 101 Marietta Street Tower, Atlanta, GA
Architect: Cooper Carry and Associates
Ink and watercolor, 17 x 12
Formal category

Marc L'Italien
L'Italien Architecture + Design

Project: Exploris—Raleigh Children's Museum, Raleigh, NC
Architect: Esherick Homsey Dodge and Davis in association with Clearscapes
Client: Exploris/County of Wake
Ink on bond, 5 x 5
Informal category

Esteban R. Latorre

Project: Twin Harbors Resort Tiki Bar, Key Largo, FL
Architect: Brown Demandt Architects
Client: Twin Harbors Resort
Pen and ink, 17 x 22
Formal category

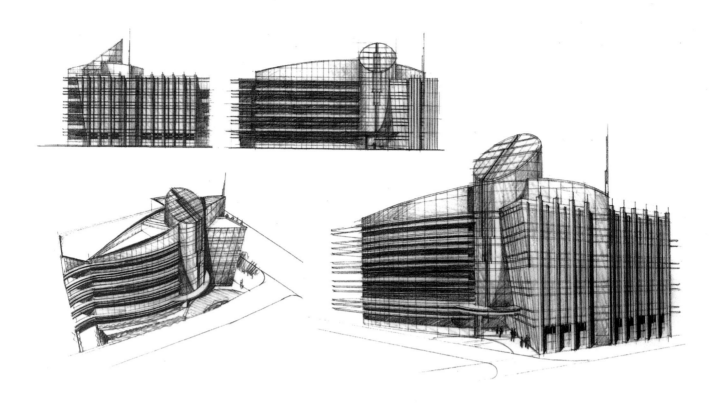

Lawrence Ko Leong
Architectural Concept Imaging

Project: Korea Medical Office Building Competition Study, Seoul, South Korea
Architect: Kaplan McLaughlin Diaz/Herbert McLaughlin
Hand-drawn prismacolor pencil/digital composite images, 20 x 30
Informal category

Laura Clayton Linn
Hellmuth, Obata + Kassabaum

Project: St. Louis City Justice Center, St. Louis, MO
Architect: Hellmuth, Obata + Kassabaum with Kennedy Associates
Client: Joe Kuss, St. Louis Board of Public Services
Watercolor, 9 x 12
Formal category

Ronald J. Love
Ronald J. Love Architectural Illustration

Project: Forest Sciences Centre
University of British Columbia, Vancouver, Canada
Architect: Dalla-Lana/Griffin Architects
Pen, ink, watercolor, 25 x 15
Formal category

David Maglaty
David Maglaty, Architect

Project: Village Center, Sequoia National Park, CA
Architect: Esherick Homsey Dodge and Davis
Client: The National Park Service
Pen and ink, 14 x 18
Informal category

Michael McCann

Project: Biscayne Bay Development, Miami Heat Arena, Miami, FL
Urban planner: Cooper/Robertson
Architect: Arquitectonica
Client: Miami Heat Development
Watercolor, 10 x 30
Informal category

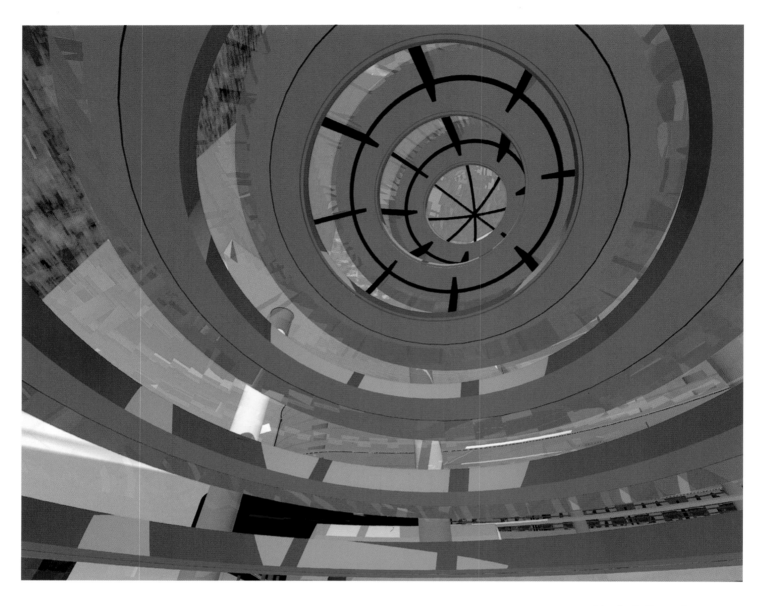

Mark S.C. Nelson AIA
Nelson Design Visuals

Project: Arts Club of Chicago Proposal, Rotunda, Chicago, IL
Architect: Mark S.C. Nelson AIA
Client: Nelson Design
Digital mapping and modeling, 14 x 18
Informal category

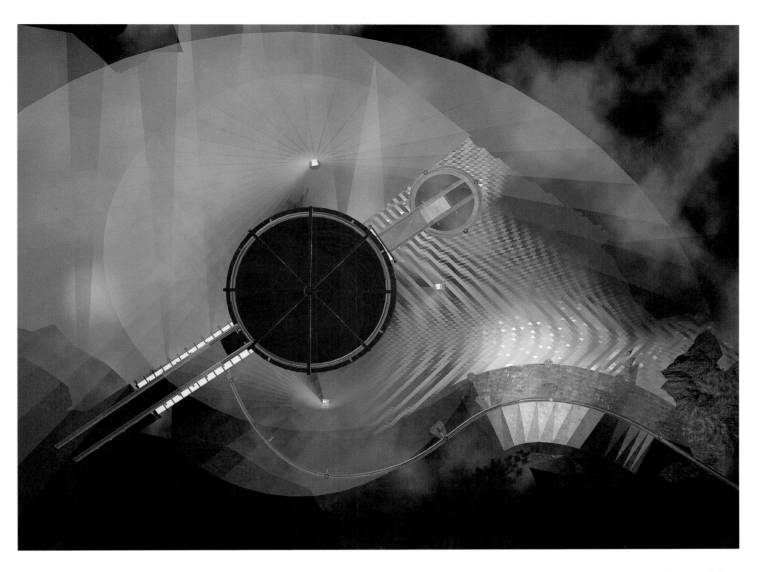

David S. Nobles
Impulse Images & Animations

Project: Fortress Garden: Plan View
Architect: David Nobles
Client: Self-commissioned
Computer, 23 x 30
Formal category

Informal category

TOWER STUDY @ USCG CHINC,   11/21

Wesley L. Page AIA

Project: Tower Study, Coast Guard Station, Chincoteague, VA
Architect: Hanbury Evans Newill Vlattas & Company
Client: United States Coast Guard
Prismacolor and marker on vellum, 6 x 5
Informal category

Payne Rowlett

Project: 600 Thirteenth Street Lobby, Washington, DC
Architect: Robert A. M. Stern Architects
Client: Deutsche Immobilien Fonds AG and Hines
Computer, 24 x 30
Formal category

Wilbur Pearson
Wilbur Pearson, Architect/Perspectivist

Project: Private Residence, Jackson, MS
Architect: Ken Tate, Architect
Pencil on 1000H tracing paper, 13 x 20
Formal category

Eugene V. Radvenis
E. V. Radvenis

Project: Chan Centre Concert Theatre, Vancouver, Canada
Architect: Bing Thom Architects
Client: University of British Columbia
Computer image, 12 x 15
Formal category

Michael Reardon
Michael Reardon Architectural Illustration

Project: Roxas Triangle Towers, Manila, Philippines
Architect: Skidmore Owings & Merrill, San Francisco, CA
Watercolor, 24 x 15

Formal category

Samuel C. Ringman
Ringman Design and Illustration

Project: Cascade House
Architect: Ringman Design and Illustration
Client: Self-commissioned
Watercolor, 6 x 6
Informal category

Ron Rose
Art Associates

Project: Ski Resort, Utah
Architect: Ron Rose, designer
Client: Self-commissioned
Casein, 15 x 19
Formal category

Thomas W. Schaller AIA
Schaller Architectural Illustration

Project: Columbus Circle Redevelopment Competition, New York, NY
Architect: James Stewart Polshek & Partners with Gary Handel & Associates
Client: The Millennium Partnership
Watercolor and pencil, 17 x 11
Formal category

Tom Sherrill
Caperton Johnson

Project: James Residence Entry, Dallas, TX
Architect: Caperton Johnson
Client: Otis & Gretchen James
Felt tip pen on vellum, 11 x 11
Informal category

Rael D. Slutsky AIA
Rael D. Slutsky & Associates

Project: New Terminal—Beirut International Airport, Beirut, Lebanon
Architect: Perkins & Will Architects
Client: Mid-East Airlines
Pen and ink, color pencil and pastel, 11 x 17
Formal category

Henry E. Sorenson Jr.

Project: Boathouse, Temperate River Landscape
Architect: Henry Sorenson
Client: Self-commissioned
Watercolor, 4 x 6
Informal category

Stanislaw W. Szroborz
Atelier Szroborz

Project: Study III, Wiesbaden, Germany
Architect: Grimbacher & Partner
Client: Grimbacher & Partner
Pen and markers, 17 x 12
Informal category

Mongkol Tansantisuk AIA
Architectural Presentations

Project: Indiana Historical Society
Architect: The Stubbins Associates
Client: Indiana Historical Society
Wax-based pencil, 10 x 17
Formal category

Willem van den Hoed
1000 HUIZEN

Project: Language University, Geneva, Switzerland
Architect: Robert Schimmelpenninck
Digital retouch on AutoCad screen dump, 1200 x 800 (pixels)
Informal category

Koji Watanabe

Project: Hotel Keihan Temmabashi Project, Osaka, Japan
Architect: Takenaka Corporation
Client: Keihan Electric Railway Co., Ltd.
Watercolor, 28 x 19
Formal category

Curtis James Woodhouse

Project: Sasson Hotel, Miami Beach, FL
Architect: Schapiro Associates
Client: SKIP Properties
Watercolor, 20 x 14

Formal category

Xu Xiaoping

Project: Jitic Office Building, Nanjing, China
Architect: Mitchell M. Gao Associate AIA
Client: Architecture Research Institute of Southeast University
Gouache airbrush, 30 x 20

Formal category

Masaaki Yamada
Nikken Sekkei , Ltd.

Project: "S" Redevelopment Project, Toyko, Japan
Architect: Nikken Sekkei
Transparent watercolor, 11 x 15
Formal category

Fujio Yoshida
Pers Pranning

Project: Osaka Station Renewal Proposal, Osaka, Japan
Architect: Pers Pranning
Airbrush, pen and ink, 22 x 27
Formal category

Serge Zaleski FSAI ARAIA
Delineation Graphix

Project: Finger Wharves Redevelopment, Sydney, Australia
Architect: Denton Corker Marshall Architects
Client: Kerry Packer/David Mariner
Tempera, 24 x 36
Formal category

Andrzej Zarzycki

Project: Philippines Medical Center, Cavite, Philippines
Architect: TRO/The Ritchie Organization
Client: New England Consortium
Computer graphics, 10 x 16
Formal category

Aaron K. Zimmerman
WRS Architects

Project: Save A Connie Air Museum, Kansas City, MO
Architect: WRS Architects
Client: Save A Connie
Computer generated, 18 x 24
Formal category

Designated Entries

During the course of the judging, the jury members were asked to evaluate the works that were not selected for the travelling exhibition. On the following pages are the submitted works that the jury deemed exceptional enough to merit publication in the catalogue.

Addresses and telephone numbers of the Designated Entrants can be found in the Membership Directory, starting on page 136.

Keiko Akasaka *a*
Architect: Atsushi Ueda Architects & Associates

James W. Akers *b*
Akers Visualization
Architect: Rockwell Group Architects

Advanced Media Design *c*
Architect: Pei Cobb Freed & Partners
Client: University of Cincinnati

a

b

c

a

Jim Anderson *a*
Anderson Illustration Associates
Architect: Bowen Williamson Zimmermann
Client: University of Wisconsin Waisman Center

Richard C. Baehr AIA *b*
Architectural Rendering
Architect: Kohn Pederson Fox Associates P.C.
Client: Donald Trump

David Baker *c*

Michael Anderson *d*
Architect: Andrew A. Kusnierkiewicz AIA
Client: Jack Barlow Designs

Sachiko Asai *e*
Architect: Sachiko Asai
Client: Atelier Aku Corporation

b

c

d

e

a

Robert Becker *a*
Architect: Arquitectonica
Client: Discovery Science Center

Alexander Ballings *b*
7ARTS visuals bv.
Architect: Mecanoo Architects
Client: Van Huisstede Communication

Anita S. Bice *c*
Architect: Fortinberry Associates Architects
Client: NLIF

Frank Bartus *d*
Genesis Studios
Architect: Hellmuth, Obata + Kassabaum
Client: Hellmuth, Obata + Kassabaum

Susan M. Biasiolli AIA *e*
Kovert-Hawkins Architects
Architect: Kovert Hawkins Architects
Client: United States Postal Service

b

c

d

e

a

Luis Blanc *a*

Mohammed U. Bilbeisi AIA *b*

Nicholas J. Buccalo AIA *c*
The Drawing Studio
Architect: K. Roche J. Dinkeloo & Associates
Client: Hines

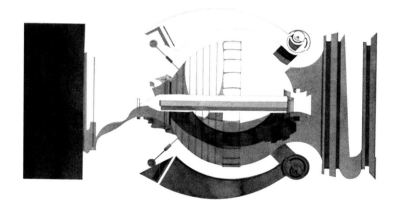

Lori Brown *d*
Lori Brown Consultants Ltd.
Architect: Webb Zerafa Menkes Housden
Client: Sealand Housing Corporation

Mona Brown *e*
Architect: Perkins & Eastman
Client: University of Connecticut

b

c

d

e

a

Li Chen *a*
Cyber Expression LLC
Architect: Keough Design
Client: AEA Investors

b

Ouxiang Chen *b*
Architect: Leo A. Daly
Client: General Services Administration

Hans K. Chao *c*
Architect: Cambridge Seven Associates
Client: Georgia

Mike Burroughs *d*
Architect: Callison Architecture

Lixian Chen *e*
Architecture Research Institute of Southeast University
Architect: Architecture Research Institute of Southeast University
Client: Quanzhou Library

c

d

QUAN ZHOU LIBRARY DESIGN

e

a

Tammy Cooper *a*
Client: Queensland Rail

Sandra Cuncu-McKinnon *b*
Robert McIlhargey & Associates
Architect: SCI Management Corporation
Client: Ocean View Chapel Cemetery

Elizabeth A. Day *c*
Elizabeth Day Architectural Illustration
Architect: Schnabli, Amman, Ruchat with Steven Fong
Client: Swiss RE America

Richard Chenoweth AIA *d*
Architectural Watercolors
Architect: Hartman-Cox Architects
Client: American University

Frank M. Costantino *e*
F. M. Costantino
Architect: Ellerbe Becket Architects

b

c

d

e

a

Angelo De Castro a
Architect: Steffen Lehmann & Partner, and
Arata/Sozaki & Associates
Client: Hanseatica Gmbh

Rafael De Jesus b
Architect: The Leblond Partnership

James F. Earl c
Earl Design
Architect: KZF
Client: Fidelity Properties

Wei Dong d

Lee A. Dunnette AIA e
Architect: Cesar Pelli & Associates

b

c

d

e

a

Peter R. Edgeley FSAI, RIBA *a*
Peter Edgeley Pty. Ltd.
Architect: Ted Ashton, E.R. Ashton Architects
Client: Fletcher Constructions

Ricardo Escajadillo *b*
Looney Ricks Kiss Architects
Architect: Looney Ricks Kiss Architects
Client: Inn Serve Corporation

Richard B. Ferrier FAIA *c*
Firm Y Architects
Architect: FirmX RB Ferrier FAIA Architect

Robert Frank *d*
Robert Frank Associates
Architect: Tanner Leddy Maytum Stacy
Client: Tanner Leddy Maytum Stacy

Wenfei Feng *e*
Leidenfrost/Horowitz & Associates
Architect: Fugleberg Koch Architects
Client: RND Developments

b

c

d

e

a

Masatoshi Fujimoto *a*
Architect: KK Kenchiku Sekkei

Jane Grealy *b*
Jane Grealy & Associates Pty. Ltd.
Architect: Bligh Voller Architects
Client: Alsons Land Corporation

Gilbert Gorski AIA *c*
Gorski & Associates, P.C.

Christopher A. Grubbs *d*
Christopher Grubbs Illustrator
Architect: Skidmore Owings Merrill

Gordon Grice OAA, MRAIC *e*
Client: Forrec Ltd.

b

c

d

e

a

Headrick Chase & Associates *a*
Architect: KTGY Group
Client: Del Webb Corporation

Mariko Hayashi *b*
A&M Co. Ltd.
Architect: Nihou Sekkei Co. Ltd.
Client: Odakyu Department Store

David Hadaway *c*

John A. Hawkins AIA *d*
Architect: Kathy Helm & Associates
Client: Kathy Helm & Associates

Bei Guan *e*
Bay Illustration Studio
Architect: The Retail Group
Client: Sears Roebuck and Company

b

c

d

Bei G 96

e

a

Andy Hickes *a*
Digital Architectural Illustration
Client: Lancome International

Brent Holly *b*

William G. Hook *c*
W. G. Hook Architectural Illustration
Architect: EDAW

Stephan Hoffpauir AIA *d*
Architect: Hellmuth, Obata + Kassabaum

Ric Heldt *e*
A & E Architects P.C.
Architect: A & E Architects P.C.
Client: Billings Depot

b

c

d

e

a

Howard R. Huizing *a*

Suns S. K. Hung *b*
Sun & Associates
Architect: Fox & Fowle Architects

John Howey *c*
Architect: John Howey Associates
Client: Mr. & Mrs. Payson Kennedy

Interface Multimedia *d*
Architect: Quinn Evans Architects
and Hartman Cox Architects
Client: J. F. K. Center for the Performing Arts

Yoshie Ideno *e*
Client: Zoo Advertisement Agency

b

c

d

e

a

Douglas E. Jamieson *a*
Architect: Gensler and Associates

Chiaki Ishida *b*
Architect: Masahiko Mizuno Mephist
Client: Joy International

Andrew Kalback *c*
Architect: LDR International

David E. Joyner *d*
Presentation Techniques
Architect: David E. Joyner

Sven Johnson *e*
Architect: Manning Silverstein Architects
Client: Carlie's Bakery

b

c

d

e

a

Young H. Ki KIA *a*
Young H. Ki & Associates
Architect: UG Architects, Young H. Ki &
Associates, Embiance
Client: UG Architects

Toshiro Kamezaki *b*
Key Design
Architect: Oka
Client: Mie Pref

Wataru Katoh *c*
Architect: Shimizu Corporation
Client: Shimizu Corporation

Byoung Sun Kang *d*
Architect: Byoung Sun Kang
Client: Sam Sung Ltd.

Takuji Kariya *e*
RIYA Co., Ltd.
Architect: Kan Izue Architects & Associates

b

c

d

e

a

Hisao Konishi *a*
Studio ARG
Architect: Raymond Woo & Associates
Client: T.A.D.

Joseph C. Knight *b*
Knight Architects
Architect: Cooper Carry and Associates

Sadako Kinuta *c*
Architect: Takenaka Corporation
Client: Kondou Corporation

Hyon Chol Kim *d*
Architect: Wimberly Allison Tong & Goo

Robert J. Kirchman *e*
Kirchman Associates
Architect: Henry Browne, Architect
Client: Caleb Stowe Associates

b

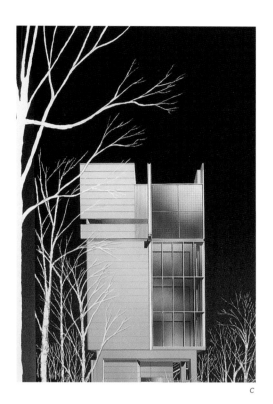

c

d

e

a

Sun Ho Lee *a*

Lawrence Ko Leong *b*
Architecture Concept Imaging
Architect: Architecture International

Esteban R. Latorre *c*
Architect: Brown Demandt Architects
Client: Sugar Loaf Key

Marc L'Italien *d*
L'Italien Architecture + Design
Architect: L'Italien Architecture + Design

Jens R. Lerback *e*
Architectural Illustrations
Architect: FFA Architects
Client: National Park Service

b

c

d

e

a

Charles R. Manus a
Architectural Presentation Arts
Architect: Foil Wyatt Architects

Laura Clayton Linn b
Hellmuth, Obata + Kassabaum
Architect: Hellmuth Obata + Kassabaum

Ronald J. Love c
Ronanld J. Love Architectural Illustration
Architect: James KM Cheng

David Maglaty d
David Maglaty, Architect
Architect: Esherick Homsey Dodge and Davis
Client: Department of General Services

Michael Mao e
RTKL Associates
Architect: RTKL Associates
Client: General Growth Properties

b

c

d

e

a

Yasuko Matsuda *a*
Architect: Takenaka Corporation

Michael McCann *b*
Architect: National Capital Planning Commission

Gretchen Maricak *c*

Alan Maskin *d*
Olson Sundberg Architects
Architect: Olson Sundberg Architects
Client: John Barutt

John P. Margolis AIA *e*
Margolis, Inc.
Architect: Margolis, Inc.

b

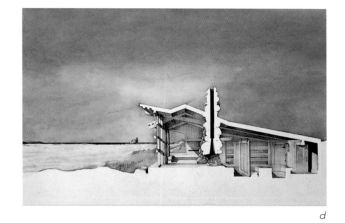

d

c

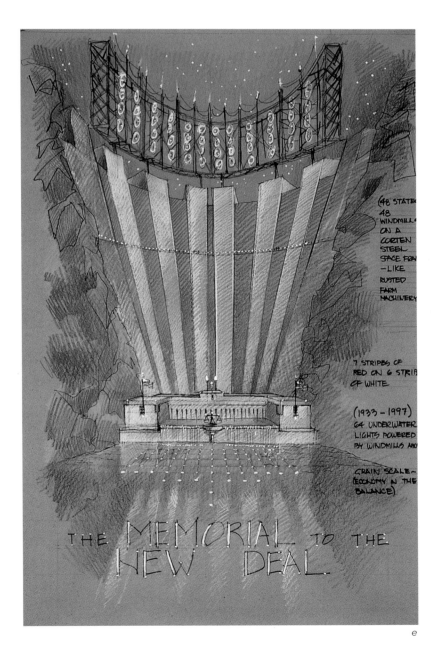

(48 STATE
48
WINDMILL
ON A
CORTEN
STEEL
SPACE FRA
—LIKE
RUSTED
FARM
MACHINERY

7 STRIPES OF
RED ON 6 STRIP
OF WHITE

(1933 – 1997)
64 UNDERWATER
LIGHTS POWERED
BY WINDMILLS ABO

GRAIN SCALE–
(ECONOMY IN THE
BALANCE)

THE MEMORIAL TO THE
NEW DEAL

e

a

Ayako Mochizuki *a*
Architect: Takenaka Corporation

Robert McIlhargey *b*
Robert McIlhargey & Associates, Ltd.
Architect: Stuart Howard Architect
Client: Milborne Real Estate

Jurgen Mehnert *c*
Architect: Architekten RKW & Partnership
Client: Competition

Brian McFarland *d*
Architect: Fink, Roberts, and Petrie
Client: Indianapolis Motor Speedway

Norihiro Morita *e*
Nomura Co. Ltd.

b

c

d

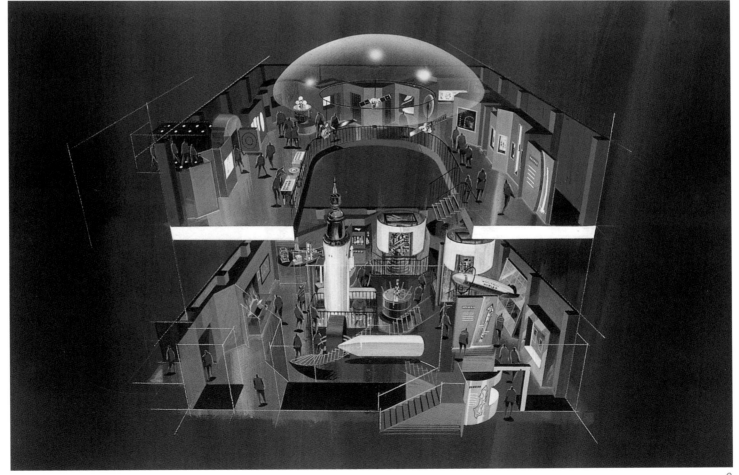

e

a

Michael B. Morrissey *a*
Michael B. Morrissey & Company
Architect: Dunlop Farrow Architects

David S. Nobles *b*
Impulse Images & Animations
Architect: David Nobles

Mark S. C. Nelson AIA *c*
Nelson Design Visuals
Architect: Mark S. C. Nelson AIA

John Naggs *d*
Architect: Peddle Thorp Architects

Martin J. Newton *e*
Archimation
Client: Tishman Speyer Metodo

b

c

d

e

a

Wesley L. Page AIA a
Architect: Hanbury Evans Newill Vlattas & Co.
Client: Virginia Tech

Kay N. Onwukwe b
Architect: HKI Associates
Client: ODNR-Division of Engineering

Les Ollenberg c
Odin Creative Dimensions
Client: Banff National Park

b

Shin Ozawa d
Architect: Shimizu Corporation
Client: Shimizu Corporation

Steve Parker AIA e
Parker Studios
Architect: Hellmuth Obata + Kassabaum
Client: Hellmuth Obata + Kassabaum

c

d

e

a

Eugene V. Radvenis *a*
E. V. Radvenis
Architect: Arthur Erickson Architectural
Corporation, and Nick Milkovich Architects
Client: Bukit Cahaya Country Resorts

Payne Rowlett *b*
Architect: Robert A. M. Stern Architects
Client: Deutsche Immobilien Fonds AG

Wilbur Pearson *c*
Wilbur Pearson, Architect/Perspectivist
Architect: Ken Tate, Architect

Merike Phillips *d*
B. Phillips/M. Phillips Architectural Illustration
Architect: Kahler Slater
Client: Kahler Slater

b

Barbara Worth Ratner AIA *e*
Architect: Marvel Flores Cobian & Asociados
Client: Comision Pro Sede Olimpiana

c

d

e

a

Travis L. Rice *a*
RDG Crose Gardner Shukert
Architect: Travis Rice
Client: Simpson College

Ron Rose *b*
Art Associates
Architect: Fullerton Diaz
Client: Plaza Properties

Michael Reardon *c*
Michael Reardon Architectural Illustration
Architect: Sasaki Associates

Samuel C. Ringman *d*
Ringman Design and Illustration
Architect: Ringman Design and Illustration

Eamon Regan *e*
Architect: Simon J. Kelly & Associates Architects
Client: Galway Tourist Board Offices

b

d

c

e

a

Eric C. Schleef *a*
Eric Schleef Illustration
Architect: Schenkel Shultz
Client: Schenkel Shultz

Thomas W. Schaller AIA *b*
Schaller Architectural Illustration
Architect: Frank Lloyd Wright and others
Client: Otis Elevator

Al Rusch AIA *c*
Phillips Swager Associates
Architect: Phillips Swager Associates
Client: Edward Hospital

Joyce Rosner *d*
The Rosner Studio
Architect: Sharon Tyler Hoover
Client: Sharon Tyler Hoover

Philip Sampson *e*
Leo A. Daly
Architect: Leo A. Daly
Client: Strategic Air Command

b

c

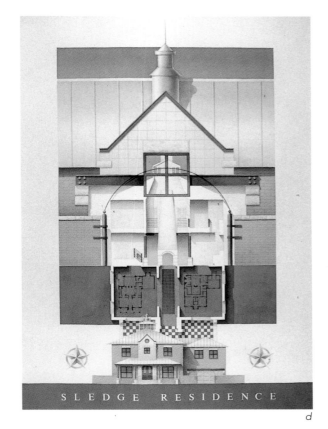

SLEDGE RESIDENCE

d

e

a

Kazuko Shimada *a*
Architect: Kiko Mozuna
Client: Public Office of Toyama Prefecture

Lynn Shimamoto *b*
Architect: Jensen Douglas Architects
Client: Echo Bay Alaska

Brian Seufert *c*
Architect: All, The World of Architects' Realities
Client: Anyone who will imagine
with us in pespective

Tom Sherrill *d*
Caperton Johnson
Architect: Caperton Johnson

George A. Schneider *e*
Watercolors By Schneider

b

c

d

e

a

Rael D. Slutsky AIA *a*
Rael D. Slutsky & Associates
Architect: Perkins & Will
Client: University of Illinois

Henry E. Sorenson Jr. *b*

James C. Smith *c*
The Studio of James C. Smith

Hisae Shoda *d*
Architect: Naoyuki Nagat, Shinji Ikada,
Yuji Shimizu/ICU
Client: Watanabe

Dick Sneary *e*
Sneary Architectural Illustration
Architect: HNTB
Client: HNTB

b

c

d

e

a

Peter Szasz *a*
Peter Szasz Associates
Architect: Field/Paoli

Masakazu Takahata *b*
Architect: Takenaka Corporation
Client: Hanshin Electric Railway

Stanislaw W. Szroborz *c*
Atelier Szroborz
Architect: RKW Architects Dusseldorf
Client: RKW Architects Dusseldorf

Yelena Stepanvants *d*
The Stellar Group
Architect: The Stellar Group

Dario Tainer AIA *e*
Tainer Associates, Ltd.
Architect: Tainer Associates

b

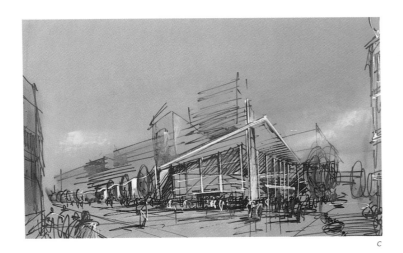

c

d

e

a

Yuji Takai *a*
Architect: Sumitomo Corporation, Architects
Client: Madra

Sergei E. Tchoban *b*
NPS und Partner
Architect: Nietz Prasch Sigl & Partner
Client: Bull & Dr. Liedfke

Mongkol Tansantisuk AIA *c*
Architectural Presentations

Rene Thibault *d*
Thibault Illustrations Ltd.

Akihide Tsurumaki *e*
Takenaka Corporation
Architect: Takenaka Corporation
Client: Saitama-ken

b

c

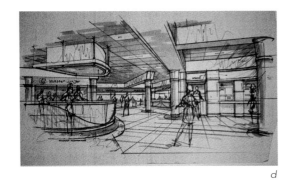

d

e

a

Theo van Leur a

Theo van Leur Architectuur Presentaties B.V.
Architect: Gunnar Daan Architectuur B.V.
Client: Slokker Uastgoed B.V.

Willem van den Hoed b

1000 HUIZEN
Architect: Alquin Olthof

Jerome Unterreiner Jr. c

Architect: Zimmer Gunsul Frasca Partnership

Mark Ueland AIA d

Ueland, Junker & McCauley, Architects
Architect: Ueland, Junker & McCauley, Architects

Masanari Wakita JARA e

Architect: Takenaka Corporation

b

c

d

e

a

Wendy L. White *a*
Wendy L. White Illustrator
Architect: Arthur Erickson

Koji Watanabe *b*
Architect: Cesar Pelli & Associates, Takenaka Corp.
Client: Keihan Electric Railway Company Ltd.

Robert G. Watel Jr. *c*
Watel Design Communication

Andrew S. K. Wee *d*
Architect: Architects 61 Pte Ltd.

Degang Wang *e*
Architect: Degang Wang, W to the Power Architects
Client: Crown Decoration Engineering Company

b

c

d

THE PERSPECTIVE OF L.R

e

d

Reiko Yamamoto a
Architect: Shimizu Corporation
Client: Shimizu Corporation

Xu Xiaoping b
Architecture Research Institute of Southeast University
Client: Architecture Research Institute of Southeast University

Curtis James Woodhouse c
Architect: Perez & Perez

Masaaki Yamada d
Nikken Sekkei Ltd.
Architect: Nikken Sekkel Ltd.

John C. Womack AIA e
OSU School of Architecture
Architect: John C. Womack AIA

b

c

d

e

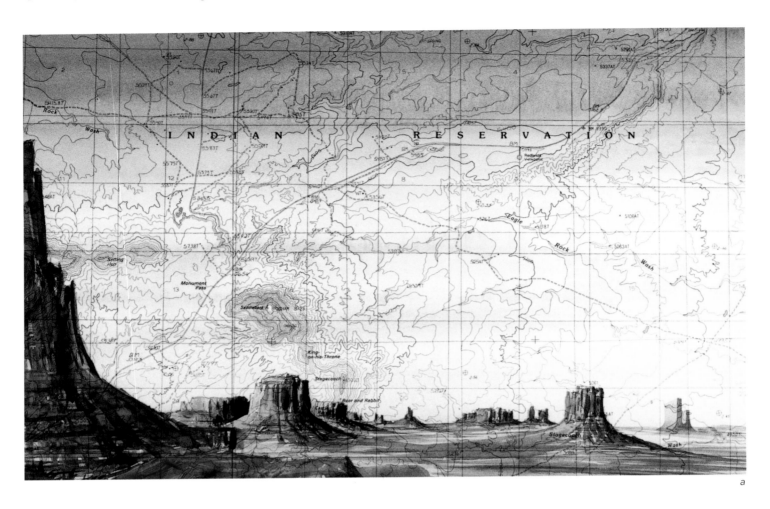

a

Tamotsu Yamamoto *a*

Jerry Yin *b*
NBBJ
Architect: NBBJ
Client: NBBJ

Tomoko Yoshimura *c*
Architect: Cesar Pelli & Associates, Takenaka Corporation
Client: Keihan Electric Railway Co. Ltd.

Kazunori Yoshimoto JARA *d*
Takenaka Corporation
Architect: Takenaka Corporation
Client: K Corporation

Fujio Yoshida *e*
Pers Pranning
Architect: Fujio Yoshida

b

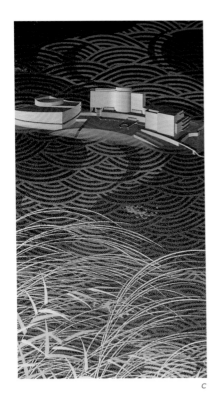

c

d

e

a

Serge Zaleski FSAI, ARAIA *a*
Delineation Graphix
Architect: Denton Corker Marshall
Client: Denton Corker Marshall

Andrzej Zarzycki *b*
Architect: TRO/The Ritchie Organization
Client: New England Consortium

Aaron K. Zimmerman *c*
WRS Architects
Architect: WRS Architects
Client: Save-A-Connie

b

c

Advanced Media Design
14 Imperial Place, Suite 202B
Providence, RI 02903
401-272-1637
Fax: 401-272-6240

Akasaka, Keiko
102 Casa, 33 Minami-Ichijo-cho Daishogun
Kita-ku, Kyoto 603
Japan
81-75-464-2460
Fax: 81-75-464-2460

Akers, James W.
Akers Visualization
20 Prospect Street
Summit, NJ 07901
908-273-8714
Fax: 908-277-0578

Alessi, Lawrence
15376 Deering
Livonia, MI 48154
313-266-6083

Anderson, Jim
Anderson Illustration Associates
1435 East Main Street
Madison, WI 53703
608-251-2025
Fax: 608-255-7750

Anderson, Michael
22 Howard Drive
Belleville, IL 62223
618-538-5622
Fax: 618-538-5622

Asai, Sachiko
563 Ishiyama Minami-ku
Sapporo, Hokkaido 005
Japan
81-11-591-1683
Fax: 81-11-591-9519

Atsuko, Hisatsune
Nishihara 1-10-7-301
Asaka, Saitama 351
Japan
81-48-487-3572

Baehr, Richard C., AIA
Architectural Rendering
305 Northern Boulevard
Great Neck, NY 11021
516-466-0470
Fax: 516-466-1670

Baker, David
2000 Huntington Avenue, #1117
Alexandria, VA 22303
703-317-3875

Ballings, Alexander
7ARTS visuals bv.
Wouwerbroek 17
5122 GV Rijend
The Netherlands
31-161-226-954
Fax: 31-161-226-457

Bartus, Frank
Genesis Studios
225 South Swoope Avenue, Suite 205
Maitland, FL 32751
407-539-2606
Fax: 407-644-7901

Becker, Robert
2337 Balboa Street
San Francisco, CA 94121
415-752-9946
Fax: 415-752-9947

Biasiolli, Susan M., AIA
Kovert- Hawkins Architects
630 Walnut Street
Jeffersonville, IN 47130
812-282-9554
Fax: 812-282-9171

Bice, Anita S.
1009 Park Avenue
Moody, AL 35004
205-640-6168
Fax: 205-640-6168

Bilbeisi, Mohammed U., AIA
2022 West University Avenue
Stillwater, OK 74074
405-377-4748
Fax: 405-377-4748

Bird, Mark D.
Power Graphics
11701 Commonwealth Drive
Louisville, KY 40299
502-267-0772
Fax: 502-267-8792

Blanc, Luis
30 St. Felix Street, #3A
Brooklyn, NY 11217
718-797-1267
Fax: 718-522-1511

Bracken, Edward J.
11809 Woodland View Drive
Fredericksburg, VA 22407
540-786-3829
Fax: 540-786-1373

Brinson, J. David, AIA
Brinson & Betts, AIA Architects
7948 Goodwood Boulevard
Baton Rouge, LA 70806
504-926-5045
Fax: 504-926-5046

Broland, Kathryn
88 Pendleton Lane
Londonderry, NH 03053
603-432-0736

Brown, Lori
Lori Brown Consultants Ltd.
1639 West 2nd Avenue, #410
Vancouver, BC V6J 1H3
Canada
604-736-7897
Fax: 604-736-9763

Brown, Mona
7 Bonnie Brook Lane
Westport, CT 06880
203-222-8088
Fax: 203-222-0726

Brown, Stephen A.
110 Lakeview Avenue
Waltham, MA 02154
617-367-6300
Fax: 617-742-8722

Buccalo, Nicholas J., AIA
The Drawing Studio
211 Warren Street
Brooklyn, NY 11201
718-488-7894
Fax: 718-488-7894

Burroughs, Mike
530 NE Ryen Street
Poulsbo, WA, 98370
360-394-2281
Fax: 360-394-2282

Cermak, Dianne S.P.
The Book-Lined Room
34 Glendoon Road
Needham, MA, 02192
617-455-6334
Fax: 617-433-0839

Chao, Hans K.
101 Western Avenue, #54
Cambridge, MA 02139
617-497-9924

Chen, Li
Cyber Expression LLC
69-23 173rd Street
Flushing, NY 11365
718-380-0669
Fax: 718-969-5363

Chen, Lixian
Architecture Research Institute of
Southeast University
Nanjing, Jiangsu 210096
China
86-25-6647433

Chen, Ouxiang
2912 East Indian School Road, A-209
Phoenix, AZ 85016
602-954-0818
Fax: 602-381-1456

Chenoweth, Richard, AIA
Architectural Watercolors
518 Margaret Drive
Silver Spring, MD 20910
301-588-0528
Fax: 301-589-0336

Christensen, Verne
Christensen Architectural Illustration
20900 West 105
Olathe, KS 66061
913-764-3803
Fax: 913-829-6479

Church, Ron
30280 Southfield Road, #114
Southfield, MI 48076
810-594-6754

Collins, James
Collins Graphics & Illustration
207 North Broadway, Suite 503
Billings, MT 59101
406-248-8988
Fax: 406-248-2735

Compton, Kristen P.
13947 Riverwood
Sterling Heights, MI 48312
810-268-2136

Cooper, Chad
1320 Creekside Drive, #1503
Norman, OK 73071
405-573-9106

Cooper, Tammy
395 Chatsworth Road
Coorparoo Brisbane, QLD 4151
Australia
61-7-3394-4333
Fax: 61-7-3849-0646

Costantino, Frank M.
F.M. Costantino
13B Pauline Street
Winthrop, MA 02152
617-846-4766
Fax: 617-846-8720

Cuncu-McKinnon, Sandra
Robert McIlhargey & Associates
1639 West 2nd Avenue, #410
Vancouver, BC V6J 1H3
Canada
604-736-7897
Fax: 604-736-9763

Dabrowska, Alina M.
822-3130, 66 Avenue SW
Calgary, ALB T3E 5K8
Canada
403-249-7008

Dawson, William H.
9 Fieldcrest Court
Peekskill, NY 10566
914-739-2404

Day, Elizabeth A.
1218 Baylor Street, #204
Austin, TX 78703
512-469-6011
Fax: 512-469-6020

De Castro, Angelo
Rua do Alto da Milha, 50-A
Sao Joao do Estoril 2765
Portugal
351-1-4671010
Fax: 351-1-4661648

De Jesus, Rafael
229 11th Avenue SE, #306
Calgary, AB T2G 0Y1
Canada
403-265-3304
Fax: 403-266-1992

DeWitt, Terry E.
5210 Dunnellon
Memphis, TN 38134
901-525-2557
Fax: 901-525-2570

DiVito, Kenneth, AIA
DiVito Illustrations
4347 Devonshire Drive
Troy, MI 48098
810-952-5155
Fax: 810-952-5155

Do, Tung Thanh, AIA
GMB Architects & Engineers
PO Box 2159, 145 College Avenue
Holland, MI 49422-2159
616-392-7034
Fax: 616-392-2677

Don, Lauren A.
Bedrock Themes
3800 Park Blvd., #200
Oakland, CA 94602-1114
510-482-8800
Fax: 510-482-8817

Dong, Wei
1300 Linden Drive
Madison, WI 53706
608-262-8805
Fax: 608-262-5335

Dozal, Peter
3502 East Camelback Road
Phoenix, AZ 85018
602-957-8979

Dragescu, Paul
27306 Midway
Dearborn Heights, MI 48127

Dunnette, Lee A., AIA
430 East 20th Street, #5B
New York, NY 10009
212-260-4240
Fax: 212-353-2305

Earl, James F.
Earl Design
17 Parkview Drive
Hingham, MA 02043
617-749-7982

Ebner, Mark
55 Adams Lk., #6
Waterford, MI 48235
810-738-6071

Edgeley, Peter R., FSAI, RIBA
Peter Edgeley Pty. Ltd.
30 Queens Lane, #17
Melbourne, VIC 3004
Australia
61-3-9866-6620
Fax: 61-3-9866-6621

Elabd, Samir
Truex deGroot Collins Architects
209 Battery Street
Burlington, VT 05401
802-658-2775

Escajadillo, Ricardo
Looney Ricks Kiss Architects
88 Union Avenue, #900
Memphis, TN 38103
901-521-1440
Fax: 901-525-2760

Evans, George W.
6517 Shady Valley Drive
Flowery Branch, GA 30542
404-609-9330
Fax: 404-609-9308

Eversole, James T.
5591 Pleasant Avenue
Fairfield, OH 45014
513-829-3573

Feng, Wenfei
Leidenfrost/Horowitz & Associates
1833 Victory Boulevard
Glendale, CA 91201
818-246-6050
Fax: 818-240-0430

Ferrier, Richard B., FAIA
Firm Y Architects
1629 Connally Terrace
Arlington, TX 76010
817-469-0605
Fax: 817-272-5098

Fisher, Brian
Presentation Arts
P.O. Box 258
Vashon Island, WA 98070
206-567-4419
Fax: 206-463-4747

Frank, Robert
Robert Frank Associates
2858 Sacramento Street
San Francisco, CA 94115
415-749-1418
Fax: 415-749-1418

Fujimoto, Masatoshi
19-7 Sho Shikito-cho
Himeji, Hyogo-ku 671-02
Japan
81-792-53-1532
Fax: 81-792-53-1530

Garnett, Ronald L.
11635 Sedgemore Drive South
Jacksonville, FL 32223
904-791-4500
Fax: 904-791-4697

George, Jeffrey Michael
Jeffrey Michael George Design
934 La Barbera Drive
San Jose, CA 95126
408-292-3041
Fax: 408-292-3044

Glen, Roderick C.
Roderick Design & Illustration
PO Box 3030
Norwood, SA 5067
Australia
61-8-8364-6866
Fax: 61-8-8364-6877

Gohl, Roger
Roger Gohl Design Studio
2643 Stoner Avenue
Los Angeles, CA 90064
310-479-0754
Fax: 310-479-4454

Gorman, Paul
801 79th Street, #304
Darien, IL 60561
630-887-8483

Gorski, Gilbert, AIA
Gorski & Associates P.C.
6633 Spokane Avenue
Lincolnwood, IL 60646
847-329-1340
Fax: 847-329-9321

Grealy, Jane
Jane Grealy & Associates Pty. Ltd.
322 Old Cleveland Road, #7
Coorparoo Brisbane, QLD 4151
Australia
61-7-3394-4333
Fax: 61-7-3849-0646

Grice, Gordon OAA, MRAIC
35 Church Street, #205
Toronto, ON M5E 1T3
Canada
416-536-9191
Fax: 416-696-8866

Grubbs, Christopher A.
Christopher Grubbs Illustrator
601 Fourth Street, #112
San Francisco, CA 94107
415-243-4394
Fax: 415-243-4395

Guan, Bei
Bay Illustration Studio
1332 229th Place NE
Redmond, WA 98053
206-868-4280
Fax: 206-868-4280

Hadaway, David
2326 West 21st Avenue
Vancouver, BC V6L 1J7
Canada
604-731-0665
Fax: 604-662-4062

Hamersky, Bohdan C.
PO Box 204
Palisades, NY 10964
212-675-0400
Fax: 212-620-4687

Harmon, Dan U.
Dan Harmon & Associates
2089 McKinley Road NW
Atlanta, GA 30318
404-609-9330
Fax: 404-609-9308

Hawkins, John A., AIA
630 Walnut Street
Jeffersonville, IN 47130
812-282-9554
Fax: 812-282-9171

Hayashi, Mariko
A&M Co. Ltd.
4-16-3 Owada
Ichikawa, Chiba 272
Japan
81-47-377-3031
Fax: 81-47-377-3077

Headrick Chase & Associates
31726 Rancho Viejo Road, #101
San Juan Capistrano, CA 92675
714-661-1955
Fax: 714-661-2898

Heldt, Ric
A & E Architects P.C.
608 North 29th Street
Billings, MT 59101
406-248-2633
Fax: 406-248-2427

Hickes, Andy
Digital Architectural Illustration
205 Third Avenue, #95
New York, NY 10003
212-677-8054

Hoffpauir, Stephan, AIA
640 Walavista Avenue
Oakland, CA 94610
510-272-9794
Fax: 510-272-9794

Holly, Brent
37849 Lakeshore Drive
Harrison Township, MI 48045
810-465-7912

Hook, William G.
W.G. Hook, Architectural Illustration
1501 Western Avenue, #500
Seattle, WA, 98101
206-622-3849
Fax: 206-624-1494

Howard, Richard P.
5800 Monroe Street
Sylvania, OH 43560
419-882-7131
Fax: 419-882-8710

Howey, John
101 South Franklin Street, #200
Tampa, FL 33602
813-223-5396
Fax: 813-229-1528

Huizing, Howard R.
145 South Olive Street
Orange, CA 92866
714-532-3012
Fax: 714-532-5298

Hung, Suns S.K.
Sun & Associates
445 Fifth Avenue, Suite 19F
New York, NY 10016
212-779-4977
Fax: 212-447-7277

Ideno, Yoshie
707 NK Kojimachi Quarters
7-10 Sanbancho, Chiyoda-ku, Tokyo 102
Japan
81-3-3263-4813
Fax: 81-3-3263-5130

Interface Multimedia
7003 Carroll Avenue
Takoma Park, MD 20912
301-270-4109
Fax: 301-270-9483

Ishida, Chiaki
81-6 Higashi-1, Inada
Obihiro, Hokkaido 080
Japan
81-155-48-8511
Fax: 81-155-48-8866

Jacobson, William
Cyma Studios
706 Price Street
West Chester, PA 19382-2130
610-436-1664
Fax: 610-436-3352

Jacques, Wayne John, AIA
Warren Freedenfeld & Associates
39 Church Street
Boston, MA 02116
617-338-0050
Fax: 617-426-2557

Jamieson, Douglas E.
827 1/2 Via de la Paz
Pacific Palisades, CA 90272
310-573-1155
Fax: 310-573-1685

Johnson, Sven
991 Manhattan Avenue, #3
Brooklyn, NY 11222
718-349-6978
Fax: 718-349-6978

Joyner, David E.
Presentation Techniques
PO Box 11173
Knoxville, TN 37939-1173
423-584-8334
Fax: 423-584-8334

Kalashian, Kraig J.
300 North Wyoming Avenue
North Massapequa, NY 11758
516-420-9453

Kalback, Andrew
222 Warren Avenue
Baltimore, MD 21230
410-727-8544
Fax: 301-498-5070

Kamezaki, Toshiro
Key Design
2-8-26 Marunouchi, Naka-ku
Nagoya, Aichi 460
Japan
81-52-203-8551
Fax: 81-52-203-8552

Kang, Byoung Sun
Dong Sung B/D 798-13
Mok-4-dong, Yangchun-gu
Seoul, 158-054
Korea
82-2-647-6111
Fax: 82-2-646-0772

Kariya, Takuji
RIYA Co., Ltd.
1-5-5-406 Tomobuchi-cho
Miyakojima-ku, Osaka 534
Japan
81-6-924-3637
Fax: 81-6-924-3287

Katoh, Wataru
1402 Calme Akabane
39-18 Iwabuchi-machi
Kita-ku, Tokyo 115
Japan
81-3-3901-1733

Ki, Young H., KIA
Young H. Ki & Associates
270 Washington Boulevard
Hoffman Estates, IL 60194
847-843-3389
Fax: 847-843-7080

Kim, Hyon Chol
1630 Liholiho Street, #904
Honolulu, HI 96822
808-537-1856
Fax: 808-536-8627

Kimball, Bruce W., AIA
309 East Harvard Avenue
Gilbert, AZ 85234
602-596-1976
Fax: 602-596-0153

Kinuta, Sadako
1-C7-503 Nakatomiga-oka
Nara-shi, Nara 631
Japan
81-742-47-7683

Kirchman, Robert J.
Kirchman Associates
5580 Jamestown Road
Crozet, VA 22932-9342
804-823-2663
Fax: 804-823-6010

Knight, Joseph C.
Knight Architects
4660 Village Court
Dunwoody, GA 30338
770-394-2798
Fax: 770-394-5311

Konishi, Hisao
Studio ARG
741-908 Iwagami-dori, Rokkaku Sagaru
Nakagyo-ku, Kyoto 604
Japan
81-75-802-2291
Fax: 81-75-802-5117

L'Italien, Marc
L'Italien Architecture + Design
3740 25th Street ,Suite 401
San Francisco, CA 94110
415-285-9062
Fax: 415-285-3866

Landeck, Peter Allen
812 Southgate Apartments, #12
McHenry, IL 60050
815-385-3430

Latorre, Esteban R.
11511 SW 100 Street
Miami, FL 33176
305-442-1193
Fax: 305-445-1496

Law, Candace
1864 Ellwood Avenue
Berkeley, MI 48072
810-548-9877

Lee, Sun Ho
Suk Jun Bldg., #601
364-31 Seogyo-Dong
Mapo-ku, Seoul
Korea
82-2-334-2118x7090
Fax: 82-2-338-9416

Leong, Lawrence Ko
Architectural Concept Imaging
800 27th Avenue
San Francisco, CA 94121
415-387-6528
Fax: 415-387-6528

Lerback, Jens R.
Architectural Illustrations
2314 Glen Way
Claremont, CA 91711
909-626-7098

Ley, Max
Univers GMBH
Wiesenstrasse 29
Berlin, 13357
Germany
49-30-4-690-0925
Fax: 49-30-4-690-0964

Linn, Laura Clayton
Hellmuth, Obata + Kassabaum
One Metropolitan Square
211 North Broadway, Suite 600
St. Louis, MO 63102-2733
314-421-2000
Fax: 314-421-6073

Lopez, Susan C.
Architectonic Visualizations
50 Grant Drive
Avon, CT 06001
203-673-1992

Love, Ronald J.
Ronald J. Love Architectural Illustration
3891 Bayridge Avenue
West Vancouver, BC V7V 3J3
Canada
604-922-3033
Fax: 604-922-2393

Maglaty, David
David Maglaty, Architect
112 El Cerrito Avenue
Piedmont, CA 94611
510-420-1934
Fax: 415-258-3866

Manus, Charles R.
Architectural Presentation Arts
43 Union Avenue, #1
Memphis, TN 38103
901-525-4335
Fax: 901-527-1143

Mao, Michael
RTKL Associates
2828 Routh Street, #200
Dallas, TX 75201
214-871-8877
Fax: 214-871-7023

Margolis, John P., AIA
Margolis
380 Boylston Street
Boston, MA 02116
617-859-2950
Fax: 617-267-6158

Maricak, Gretchen
1040 Chapin
Birmingham, MI 48009
810-644-3001

Marshall, Janice
21946 North Center Street
Northville, MI 48167
810-347-1194

Maskin, Alan
Olson Sundberg Architects
108 First Avenue South, 4th Floor
Seattle, WA 98104
206-624-5670
Fax: 206-624-3730

Matsuda, Yasuko
5-21-6 Katsutadai
Yachiyo, Chiba 276
Japan
81-474-83-8574
Fax: 81-474-83-8574

Maurice, G. Scott
24615 Walden Road, E
Southfield, MI 48034
810-353-7736

McCann, Michael
2 Gibson Avenue
Toronto, ON M5R 1T5
Canada
416-964-7532
Fax: 416-964-2060

McFarland, Brian
14049 Old Mill Court
Carmel, IN 46032
317-846-3461
Fax: 317-580-5778

McGowan, John Paul, AIA
1402 Kersey Lane
Potomac, MD 20854
202-337-6022
Fax: 202-337-6029

McIlhargey, Robert
Robert McIlhargey & Associates, Ltd.
1639 West 2nd Avenue, #410
Vancouver, BC V6J 1H3
Canada
604-736-7897
Fax: 604-736-7897

Mehnert, Jurgen
Gansestrasse 42
Dusseldorf 40593
Germany
49-211-711-8845

Mochizuki, Ayako
13-204 Nishiisya-danchi
1-19 Kamenoi, Meito-ku
Nagoya, Aichi 465
Japan
81-52-701-4235
Fax: 81-52-201-1252

Morga, Maria T.
2301 N Street NW
Washington, DC 20037
202-728-0430
Fax: 202-728-0430

Morgan, Don
8050 SW Valley View Court
Portland, OR 97225
505-292-4308

Morita, Norihiro
Nomura Co. Ltd.
2-2-1 Shinkiba
Kohtoh-ku, Tokyo 136
Japan
81-3-5569-5840
Fax: 81-3-5569-5498

Morris, Michael
39858 Coronation
Canton, MI 48188
313-397-7921

Morrissey, Michael B.
Michael B. Morrissey & Company
223 Indian Road Crescent
Toronto, ON M6P 2G6
Canada
416-763-1387
Fax: 416-763-5892

Moskal, Wieslaw P., AIA
5835 North Kingsdale Avenue
Chicago, IL 60646
312-236-6751
Fax: 312-782-5191

Naggs, John
8/46 Terrace Street, New Farm
Brisbane, QLD 4005
Australia
61-7-3254-1506

Nastwold, Gail
24431 Bashian
Novi, MI 48075
810-471-0160

Nelson, Mark S.C., AIA
Nelson Design Visuals
3205 South Maple Avenue
Berwyn, IL 60402-2809
708-484-2720
Fax: 708-484-2730

Newton, Martin J.
Archimation
Kantstrasse 142
Berlin 10623
Germany
49-30-312-1306
Fax: 49-30-312-1620

Nobles, David S.
Impulse Images & Animations
9310 Autumn Sunrise
San Antonio, TX 78250
210-499-4949
Fax: 210-496-6641

Nowak, Krzysztof
22-61 42nd Street, #D5
Astoria, NY 11105
718-545-8656
Fax: 718-545-8656

O'Beirne, Michael P.
175-F Centre Street, #612
Quincy, MA 02169
617-846-4766
Fax: 617-846-8720

Oelfke, Don, Jr.
Don Oelfke Design
PO Box 163746
Austin, TX 78716-3746
512-328-3381
Fax: 512-328-3381

Oles, Paul Stevenson, FAIA
Interface Architects
One Gateway Center, Suite 501 A
Newton, MA 02158
617-527-6790
Fax: 617-527-6790

Ollenberg, Les
Odin Creative Dimensions
6216 Touchwood Drive NW
Calgary, AB T2K 3L9
Canada
403-274-4866
Fax: 403-275-4713

Onwukwe, Kay N.
1900 East Broad Street
Columbus, OH 43209
617-258-5553
Fax: 614-258-5578

Ozawa, Shin
Ichiharaso 102, Konodai 1-2-15
Ichikawa, Chiba 272
Japan
81-473-73-8895
Fax: 81-473-73-8895

Page, Wesley L., AIA
120 Atlantic Street, #400
Norfolk, VA 23510
757-627-5775
Fax: 757-622-1012

Parker, Steve
Parker Studios
802 Kipling Way
Weldon Spring, MO 63304
314-939-5628
Fax: 314-939-5643

Payne Rowlett
219 Glenwood Drive
Houston, TX 77007
713-864-9041
Fax: 713-880-4437

Pearson, Wilbur
Wilbur Pearson Architect/Perspectivist
6880 SW 98th Street
Miami, FL 33156
305-667-9811

Peri, Michele
16484 Jessica
Macomb, MI 48042
810-786-6882

Perry, Betsy
RR 1 Box 47
Fowler, IL 62338
217-455-3324

Phillips, Merike
B. Phillips/M. Phillips Architectural Illustration
711 61st Street
Kenosha, WI 53143
414-658-8464
Fax: 414-658-8464

Polhemus, Rick
21211 West Ten Mile Road, #515
Southfield, MI 48075
810-204-2680

Pollock, Ricky L.
Community Planning &
Architectural Associates
6330 Quandrangle Drive, Suite 260
Chapel Hill, NC 27514
919-489-1771
Fax: 919-489-3466

Query, W. R., Jr.
4212 Kelly Elliot Road
Arlington, TX 76016
817-226-0020
Fax: 817-226-0030

Radvenis, Eugene V.
E.V. Radvenis
1639 West 2nd Avenue, #410
Vancouver, BC V6J 1H3
Canada
604-736-5430
Fax: 604-736-9763

Ratner, Barbara Worth, AIA
828 Charles Allen Drive NE
Atlanta, GA 30308
404-876-3943
Fax: 404-876-3943

Reardon, Michael
Michael Reardon Architectural Illustration
5433 Boyd Avenue
Oakland, CA 94618
510-655-7030
Fax: 510-655-7030

Regan, Eamon
Paradigm House
Dundrum Office Park
Dublin 14
Ireland
353-1-296-2471
Fax: 353-1-296-2484

Rice, Travis L.
RDG Crose Gardner Shukert
414 61st Street
Des Moines, IA 50312
515-274-4925
Fax: 515-274-6937

Rich, Stephen W., AIA
85 Main Street
Saugus, MA 01906
617-231-0951
Fax: 617-245-6293

Richardson, Scott
Richardson Illustration Studio
1048 Literary Road
Cleveland, OH 44113
216-696-6780
Fax: 216-696-6994

Ringman, Samuel C.
Ringman Design and Illustration
1800 McKinney Avenue
Dallas, TX 75201
214-871-9001
Fax: 214-871-3307

Rochon, Richard
15200 East Jefferson Avenue, Suite 102
Grosse Pointe Park, MI 48230
313-331-4410
Fax: 313-331-4408

Rodriguez, Edwin, AIA
PO Box 40590
San Juan, PR 00940-0590
787-765-1137
Fax: 787-250-6068

Rogers, Mark
1648 Shenandoah Circle
Fort Collins, CO 80525
970-223-3590

Rose, Ron
Art Associates
4635 West Alexis Road
Toledo, OH 43623
419-537-1303
Fax: 419-474-9113

Rosenthal, Rachel L.
PO Box 1678
San Luis Obispo, CA 93406
805-544-7066
Fax: 805-544-7067

Rosner, Joyce
The Rosner Studio
1335 West Bosque Loop
Bosque Farms, NM 87068
505-332-8011
Fax: 505-332-8011

Rusch, Al, AIA
Phillips Swager Associates
3622 North Knoxville Avenue
Peoria, IL 61603
309-688-9511
Fax: 309-688-6490

Rush, Richard W.
768 North Bucknell Street
Philadelphia, PA 19130
215-763-8372
Fax: 215-763-8999

Sampson, Philip
Leo A. Daly
8600 Indian Hills Drive
Omaha, NE 68114
402-391-8111
Fax: 402-391-8564

Sanchez, John J., Jr.
11706 West 197th Street
Mokena, IL 60448
708-479-0276

Sanocki, Anne
21211 West Ten Mile Road, #615
Southfield, MI 48075
310-204-3326

Schaller, Thomas W., AIA
Schaller Architectural Illustration
2112 Broadway, #407
New York, NY 10023
212-362-5524
Fax: 212-362-5719

Schleef, Eric C.
Eric Schleef Illustration
7740 Dean Road
Indianapolis, IN 46240
317-595-0016
Fax: 317-595-0016

Schneider, George A.
Watercolors By Schneider
804 South Fifth Street
Columbus, OH 43206
614-443-7014

Sedlock, Daniel
23705 Walden Court
Southfield, MI 48034
810-355-9293

Seufert, Brian
6608 Twelve Oaks Boulevard
Tampa, FL 33634-2264
813-881-9780
Fax: 813-539-0964

Sherrill, Tom
Caperton Johnson
14860 Montfort Drive, #200
Dallas, TX 75240
972-991-7082
Fax: 972-991-2578

Shimada, Kazuko
7-3-4-404 Hikarigaoka
Nerima-ku, Tokyo 179
Japan
81-3-3939-8522
Fax: 81-3-3939-8522

Shimamoto, Lynn
6320 16th Avenue NE
Seattle, WA 98115
206-522-6851
Fax: 206-527-8680

Shoda, Hisae
2-3-6-102 Shodai-Motomachi
Hirakata, Osaka 573
Japan
81-720-66-9055
Fax: 81-720-66-9055

Siberell, John
Siberell Studios
W 969 Nice Lake Road
Birchwood, WI 54817
715-354-7533
Fax: 715-354-7678

Slutsky, Rael D., AIA
Rael D. Slutsky & Associates
351 Milford Road
Deerfield, IL 60015
847-267-8200
Fax: 847-267-8226

Smith, James C.
The Studio of James C. Smith
700 South Clinton Street, #100
Chicago, IL 60607
312-987-0132
Fax: 312-987-0099

Sneary, Dick
Sneary Architectural Illustration
9728 Overhill Road
Kansas City, MO 64134
816-765-7841
Fax: 816-763-0848

Sorenson, Henry E., Jr.
702 South 14th Avenue
Bozeman, MT 59715
406-587-7113
Fax: 406-994-4257

Stach, Glenn T.
502 Progress Street, #4
Blacksburg, VA 24060
540-961-3132

Stepanvants, Yelena
The Stellar Group
2900 Hartley Road
Jacksonville, FL 32257
904-260-2900
Fax: 904-386-2481

Swenson, Richard J.
PO Box 144
New Stanton, PA 15672
412-925-6387

Szasz, Peter
Peter Szasz Associates
150 Green Street
San Francisco, CA 94111
415-982-3868
Fax: 415-781-3696

Szroborz, Stanislaw W.
Atelier Szroborz
Merowingerstrasse 120
Dusseldorf 40225
Germany
49-211-317-9693
Fax: 49-211-317-9592

Tainer, Dario, AIA
Tainer Associates, Ltd.
445 West Erie Street
Chicago, IL 60610
312-951-1656
Fax: 312-951-8773

Takahata, Masakazu
1-38-21 Kuzuha Noda
Hirakata, Osaka 173
Japan
81-720-57-4044
Fax: 81-720-55-8825

Takai, Yuji
9-11-502, 3 Chome Shinkoiwa
Katsushika-ku, Tokyo 124
Japan
81-3-3692-5012
Fax: 81-3-3692-5315

Tansantisuk, Mongkol, AIA
Architectural Presentations
672 Grove Street
Newton, MA 02162-1319
617-332-7885
Fax: 617-332-3789

Tchoban, Sergei E.
NPS und Partner
Ulmenstrasse 40
Hamburg, 22299
Germany
49-40-480-6180
Fax: 49-40-470-027

Tetzlaff, Heather
2958 Greenfield
Berkley, MI 48072
810-546-0592

Thibault, Rene
Thibault Illustrations Ltd.
5810 Patina Drive SW, #61
Calgary, AB T3H 2Y6
Canada
403-217-4650
Fax: 403-246-1823

Tsurumaki, Akihide
Takenaka Corporation
2-14-6 Kichijoji-honcho
Musasino City, Tokyo 180
Japan
81-422-20-1077
Fax: 81-422-20-1077

Ueland, Mark, AIA
Ueland, Junker & McCauley, Architects
718 Arch Street 5N
Philadelphia, PA 19106
215-440-0190
Fax: 215-440-0197

Unterreiner, Jerome, Jr.
320 SW Oak
Portland, OR 97204
503-224-3860
Fax: 503-224-2482

van den Hoed, Willem
1000 HUIZEN
Lange Geer 44
2611 PW Delft
The Netherlands
31-15-213-3382
Fax: 31-15-212-0448

van Leur, Theo
Theo van Leur Architectuur Presentaties B.V.
Stadsring 165 H
3816 DS Amersfoort
The Netherlands
31-33-472-5572
Fax: 31-33-472-7788

Wakita, Masanari, JARA
3B Residence Higashiyama
1-26 Higashi yamamoto-machi Chikusa-ku
Nagoya, Aichi 464
Japan
81-52-781-4474
Fax: 81-52-201-1252

Wakita, Osamu A.
2135 Chandeleur Drive
Rancho Palos Verdes, CA 90275
310-522-8210
Fax: 310-548-0575

Walker, Anthony
31433 Merriwood Park Drive
Livonia, MI 48152
810-476-6620

Wang, Degang
Architecture Research Institute
of Southeast University
Nanjing Jingsu 210018
China
86-25-360-3106
Fax: 86-25-360-7287

Watanabe, Koji
2-20-3 Ibukino
Izumi-shi, Osaka 594
Japan
81-725-56-7608
Fax: 81-725-56-7608

Watel, Robert G., Jr.
Watel Design Communication
202 Parkland Avenue
St. Louis, MO 63122
314-821-9285
Fax: 314-821-9285

Watts, Robert
1906 Avocado Ranch Road
El Cajon, CA 92019
619-442-6438
Fax: 619-442-6417

Wee, Andrew S.K.
453 Upper East Coast Road, #03-03
The Summit
Singapore 466501
65-226-3003
Fax: 65-227-3003

White, Wendy L.
Wendy L. White Illustrator
1355 West Fourth Avenue, #205
Vancouver, BC V6H 3YA
Canada
604-731-9366
Fax: 604-736-9763

Whitman, Peter M.
Peter M. Whitman, Architectural Illustrator
77 North Washington Street
Boston, MA 02114
617-227-2932
Fax: 617-227-8316

Womack, John C., AIA
OSU School of Architecture
101 Architecture Building
Stillwater, OK 74708
405-744-6043
Fax: 405-744-6491

Woodfield, Rebecca
7099 Spring Ridge Road
West Bloomfield, MI 48322
810-737-4544

Woodhouse, Curtis James
4141 Lybyer Avenue
Miami, FL 33133
305-663-8347
Fax: 305-663-2575

Xiaoping, Xu
Architecture Research Institute of
Southeast University
Nanjing Jiangsu 210018
China
86-25-445-5637

Yamada, Masaaki
Nikken Sekkei, Ltd.
2-1-3 Koraku
Bunkyo-ku, Tokyo 112
Japan
81-3-3813-3361
Fax: 81-3-3817 0755

Yamamoto, Reiko
Kogane Kiyoshigaoka 3-19-11
Matsudo City, Chiba-ken 270
Japan
81-473-42-2146

Yamamoto, Tamotsu
15 Sleeper Street
Boston, MA 02210
617-542-1021
Fax: 617-451-0271

Yancey, John
RTKL Associates
2828 Routh Street
Dallas, TX 75201

Yin, Jerry
NBBJ
111 South Jackson Street
Seattle, WA 98104
206-223-5168
Fax: 206-621-2300

Yip, Sing, Hwa
A & R Architectural Rendering
1216 148th Aenue
San Leandro, CA 94578
510-351-8478
Fax: 510-351-8478

Yoshida, Fujio
Pers Planning
301, 4-7-11, Zuiko
Higashi yodogawa-ku, Osaka 533
Japan
81-6-327-4947
Fax: 81-6-327-4947

Yoshimoto, Kazunori JARA
Takenaka Corporation
2-20, 4-Chome Tenjin
Chuo-ku, Fukuoka 810
Japan
81-92-711-1211
Fax: 81-92-781-5276

Yoshimura, Tomoko
21-27 Kunimatsu-cho
Neyagawa-ku, Osaka 572
Japan
81-720-22-2557

Zaleski, Serge FSAI, ARAIA
Delineation Graphix
238 Bulwara Road, Ultimo
Sydney, NSW 2007
Australia
61-2-9552-3666
Fax: 61-2-9692-9082

Zarzycki, Andrzej
41 Gorham Street
Somerville, MA 02144
617-776-3472

Zhong, Ruan
Room 401 No.40 Lane 777 Liu-Zhou Road
Shanghai 200233
China
86-21-6487-9127
Fax: 86-21-6502-0707

Zimmerman, Aaron K.
WRS Architects
120 NW Parkway
Kansas City, MO 64150
816-587-9500
Fax: 816-587-1685

Officers

Charles Manus	President	901-525-4335
Barbara Worth Ratner AIA	Vice President	404-876-3943
Jon Kletzien	Treasurer	401-272-1637
Michael Reardon	Secretary	510-655-7030
Paul Stevenson Oles FAIA	Member-at-Large	617-527-6790

Advisory Council

Robert Becker	415-752-9946
Frank M. Costantino	617-846-4766
Elizabeth A. Day	512-469-6011
Gordon Grice OAA, MRAIC	416-536-9191
William G. Hook	206-622-3849
Paul Stevenson Oles FAIA	617-527-6790
Stephen W. Rich AIA	617-231-0951
Thomas W. Schaller AIA	212-362-5524
Rael D. Slutsky AIA	847-267-8200
Dario Tainer AIA	312-951-1656
Tamotsu Yamamoto	617-542-1021

Regional Coordinators

P.S. Oles FAIA, Chairman	Boston, MA	617-527-6790
Stanley Doctor	Boulder, CO	303-449-3259
Richard B. Ferrier FAIA	Arlington, TX	817-469-0605
Jeffrey M. George	San Francisco, CA	408-292-3041
Gordon Grice OAA, MRAIC	Toronto, Canada	416-536-9191
Dan U. Harmon	Atlanta, GA	404-609-9330
Sallie Hood	Norfolk, VA	757-622-6991
William G. Hook	Seattle, WA	206-622-3849
Michael McCann	Toronto, Canada	416-964-7532
Richard Rochon	Dearborn, MI	313-331-4410
Thomas W. Schaller AIA	New York, NY	212-362-5524
Rael D. Slutsky AIA	Chicago, IL	847-267-8200
Robert G. Watel, Jr.	St. Louis, MO	314-821-9285

International Coordinators

Hans K. Chao	China	o17-492-7000
Angelo De Castro	Portugal	351-1-467-1010
Ferry Djohan	Indonesia	62-21-828-0681
Masatoshi Fujimoto	Japan	81-792-53-1532
Robert Gill	Australia	613-826-1322
Jane Grealy	Australia	61-7-3394-4333
Miguelangel Gutierrez	Mexico	525-211-1921
Young Ki	Korea	847-843-3389
Sun Ho Lee	Korea	82-2-334-2118
Dario Tainer AIA	Italy	312-951-1656
Sergei Tchoban	Germany	49-40-480-6180
Willem van den Hoed	Holland	31-15-213-3382

Executive Director

Alexandra Lee	Boston	617-951-1433x225